Collected Poems
&
Selected Translations

A. C. Jacobs

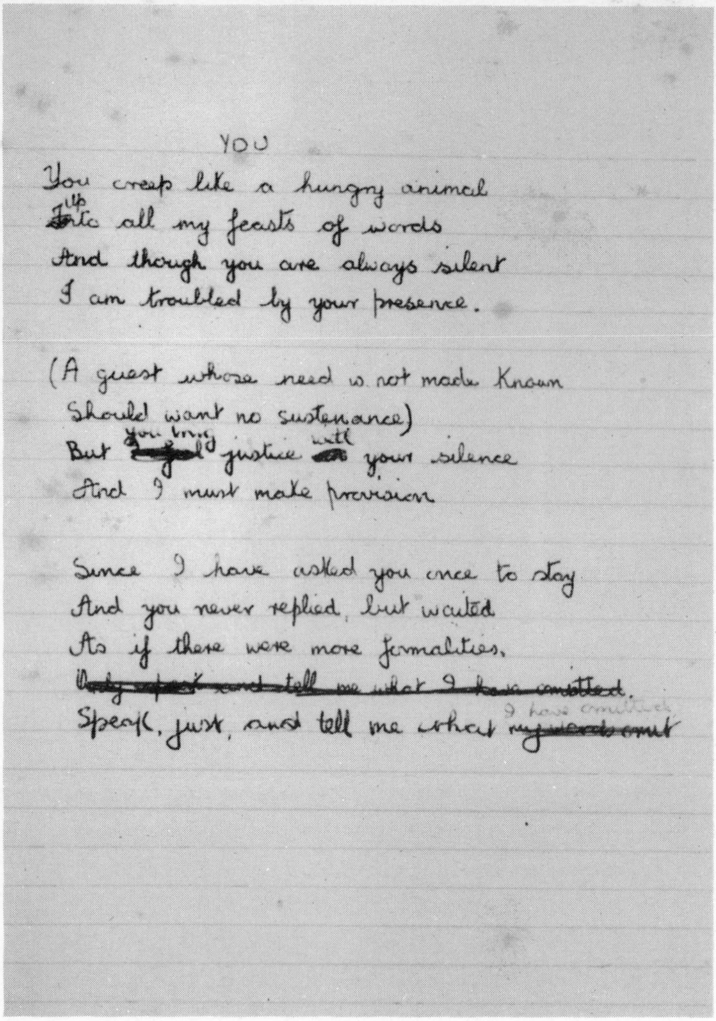

YOU

You creep like a hungry animal
~~Into~~ Up all my feasts of words
And though you are always silent
I am troubled by your presence.

(A guest whose need is not made known
Should want no sustenance)
But you bring justice with your silence
And I must make provision

Since I have asked you once to stay
And you never replied, but waited
As if there were more formalities,
~~Only speak and tell me what I have omitted.~~
Speak, just, and tell me what I have omitted

COLLECTED POEMS
&
SELECTED TRANSLATIONS

A. C. JACOBS

edited by John Rety and Anthony Rudolf
foreword by Jon Silkin

The Menard Press/Hearing Eye
(in association with the European Jewish Publication Society)

London 1996

Collected Poems & Selected Translations

A. C. Jacobs

Cover design by Audrey Jones
Design, setting and camera ready copy by Lijna Minnet
Back cover photograph by Susan Johns

Representation and distribution in UK:
Central Books (Troika)
99 Wallis Road
Hackney Wick
London E9 5LN
Tel: 0181-986 4854

Distribution in rest of the world apart from North America:
Central Books
Distribution in North America:
SPD Inc
1814 San Pablo Avenue
Berkeley CA 94702 USA

Menard: 1-874320 -10 -1
Hearing Eye: 1-870841 - 46 - 8

The Menard Press
8 The Oaks
Woodside Avenue
London N12 8AR
Tel: 0181-446 5571

Hearing Eye
Box 1
99 Torriano Avenue
London NW5 2RY

Printed by:
Arc & Throstle Press
Todmorden Lancashire

ACKNOWLEDGEMENTS

The editors wish to thank Dr Risa Domb, Lecturer in Hebrew Literature at Cambridge University, for her help concerning the translation section of this book (more details elsewhere), Frederick Grubb for his suggestions concerning chronology and interpretation, Susan Johns for her skill in deciphering Arthur Jacobs' handwriting and for other input concerning variants, Hyam Maccoby for help with some notes, Philip Hobsbaum and Jon Silkin – the two early champions of A.C.Jacobs' work – for their support and advice and, especially, their essays.

We also wish to thank Arthur's parents, Sophie and the late Moses Jacobs, his sister and brother-in-law, Sheila and Geoffrey Gilbert, and his friend Angela Fuertes, for their kind help and unstinting support.

Warm acknowledgements are due to the following for help in solving specific problems concerning poems, translations, notes and bibliography: Yehuda Amichai, Chaim Bermant, Keith Bosley, Nili Cohen, Andrew Crozier, Brian Docherty, Moshe Dor, Adam Feinstein, Robert Friend, Barbara Garvin, Timothy Gee, Martin Gilbert, Michael Hamburger, Dan Jacobson, Gabriel Levin, Deborah Maccoby and Dennis Silk.

ACKNOWLEDGEMENTS AND COPYRIGHT

Elsewhere in the book we make clear the publishing history – books, pamphlet and magazines – of the poems and translations. Here we acknowledge the magazines and publishers etc which brought out poems by A.C.Jacobs: *Acumen*, *Aquarius*, *BBC*, *Books*, *European Judaism*, *Jerusalem Post*, *Jewish Chronicle*, *Jewish Quarterly*, PEN, *Poésie Vivante*, *Cahiers Franco-Anglais*, *Poetry and Audience*, *Retrievements* (ed. Silk), *Scottish Review*, *Sixty Fives*, *Stand*, *TLS*, *Tribune*, *The Young British Poets* (ed. Robson), *Voices within the Ark* (ed. Rudolf and Schwartz), Hearing Eye, Torriano Meeting House Poetry Pamphlet Series, The Menard Press, Tim Gee Editions.

ACKNOWLEDGEMENTS FOR THE TRANSLATIONS

Some of the translations are copyright © the Institute of Hebrew Translation in Israel and the publishers are grateful to them and to the copyright holders of the original texts, as and where appropriate, for permission to include work in this volume.

Some of the translations have already appeared in the following books and magazines and the publishers wish to acknowledge this as follows:

The Vogel translations appeared as a book (along with four translations not included here), in *The Dark Gate*, The Menard Press, 1976. Some were previously published in the magazines *Modern Poetry in Translation* and *European Judaism*. Some later appeared in the anthology *Voices within the Ark*, ed. Rudolf and Schwartz, Avon Books NY, 1980.

The eleven Ben-Yitzhak translations appeared as a limited edition book published in 1994 by Tim Gee Editions. The originals were the only poems of Ben-Yitzhak to appear in Ben-Yitzhak's lifetime. Arthur Jacobs had intended to translate the remaining handful of posthumous poems but died before he could do so. The translations were previously published in *Modern Poetry in Translation* and the Israel PEN centre Bulletin. Some of them appeared in *Voices within the Ark* and *The Anthology of Modern Hebrew Poetry*, Israel Universities Press, ed. Penueli and Ukhmani 1966.

Three of the Bialik translations appeared in *Voices within the Ark*, *The Anthology of Modern Hebrew Poetry* and *Shefa Quarterly* respectively. 'On the Top of a Holy Mountain' appears to be unpublished.

The translations of Yehuda Amichai appeared in *Voices within the Ark*, *The Burning Bush*, ed. Moshe Dor, W.H.Allen 1977, *New Writing from Israel*, ed. Jacob Sonntag, Corgi 1976, and *The Jewish Chronicle*.

The translations of these eight poets appeared as follows: A.L.Strauss: *Voices within the Ark*; Amir Gilboa: *Voices*, 1969; Dahlia Ravikovitch: *Ariel*; Moshe Dor: *New Writing from Israel*; IsraelPincas: *Voices within the Ark*; Israel Hame'iri: *The Burning Bush*; Uzi Shavit: *New Writing from Israel*; Natan Zach: *New Writing from Israel*.

The translation of T. Carmi appears to be unpublished.

ARTHUR JACOBS, POET
Jon Silkin

I think I first met Arthur Jacobs in 1952 at the Ben-Uri Art Gallery, Portman Square, London, probably around the time I met Philip Hobsbaum, the novelist Louis Golding, and crucial for myself, the fiction writer and poet Emanuel Litvinoff. But it was not, I think, until 1955 that I got to know him, when we shared the top floor flat of a house owned by the novelists Bernice Rubens and Rudolf Nassauer. This was at 10 Compayne Gardens, near Finchley Road station – a house later owned by the poet and translator, Daniel Weissbort.

Pace (velocity and delay) has several guises, and what I most remember, and retain, is the slow gait of Arthur's speech expressed through a soft granular voice. This slowness was also a part of his manner and his movements, so that one would have called the pace 'deliberate' but that there was also hesitation and diffidence. His was a friendly but distinct austere energy, so distinct that although I am suspicious of making the person and the work interchangeable, thus providing a spurious basis for an apprehension of the latter, I can't escape my friendship with the poet, even if I wanted to, or separate him from his writing.

Arthur had asthma, and difficulties with breathing contributed to his hesitations of speech, but I think he would have had a delaying measured speech whatever the physiology, which in any case was perhaps as much a part of character as illness.

His speech – that's the point, I think – was both measured (an amount of certainty) and hesitant and lingering. I remember experiencing the uncomfortable contradiction of reckoning up hesitation and reluctance mixed in with authority.

I am unsure if my memory of this uncomfortable contradiction is accurate, yet I can remember that he would suddenly agree, or disagree, with such power that one felt that what had travailed through was sound judgment. I am not certain if my memory is accurate until, that is, I experience the work yet again, even though much of what I read in this book appears for the first time. That too is characteristic. He wrote with a particular certainty, yet appears to have felt unsure of what he produced. That is why, perhaps, so much remained unpublished at his death in 1994. Thus this collection.

So despite the finicking doubts about bringing together biography and work I am saying that I have a reciprocal respect for the person and the work. To claim *gravitas* for the poetry is too easy and obvious; to say it has a kind of certainty is to be slightly aside the point.

I published seven of Arthur's poems (one had been in the TLS) when I re-started *Stand* from Leeds in 1960. Copies of this issue still remain. Basis, a version of geography, seems an important component of his work, perhaps because Arthur belonged in no one place: Jewish-Glaswegian, Jewish-Israeli, Jewish-London, he lived in many locations including, lastly, Spain, the Christian version of which got rid of (most of) the Jews from its territory, after something like eleven hundred years of Moorish government, culture and relative tolerance. Arthur would have known this, and more besides. Having a minority consciousness he could site himself nowhere. There was no home, except in his speech and written language, and even in that, the poem which ought to have expressed trust expresses distrust, when he comes to write about his grandfather in 'Sovereign Penny', as the fearful contents, with their deliberate slow rhythms, show:

> I know what he wants:
> To be a proud charm on a string round my neck.
> When I tug at him for luck or breath
> I'll choke.

The almost terse ending spends on spondaic long durational (rather than stressed) syllables, yet it's not weighty or authoritative. The poem finds it has no more to say and closes, thereby implicitly showing antipathy for work that flourishes an ending. 'I'll choke'. The experience is of being obliged to trust one's forebears, and their culture, yet of being sure, as Jewish history shows, that what one would not want to shed has also the capacity to destroy one. Though this sociological reading does not allow for the personal inwardness – resentment mixed with tenderness. It is a fine, strange poem, the vitality of which issues in a doubleness of response that comes not only from being Jewish but also from its unevadable pressure upon one. Though the whole draws on an honesty that does not use one's Jewishness to evade one's personal constitution.

To hasten this complex substance, rhythmically, would be to express confidence, which is neither Arthur's mode, nor this poem's. Yet in the poem confiding in the community of poets, Jewish ones, 'In Early Spring', one reads certainty, and the rhythms tell it out, in syllables that are as often durational as those bearing the confidence of stress and accent – assertions of the ictus – in our inflected language. Oh God help us, Arthur might not at all have approved of this analysis. He might have offered 'yes' with such hesitation, reservation and doubt as to suggest that his assent would change the direction of what one had said. He had a strange and powerful hesitation:

> And I hear most the miraculous, broken poems
>
> That were made in the enclosures of insanity
> Whose authors heard the chanting of the Inquisition
> And smelt the smoke of the crematoria
> And knew there was no escape, yet wrote
> To show how life is at the verges of humanity.
>
> Their great sound grew, and in that company
> I walked past the pond and down the hill,
> Aware that nothing was ended. With this Spring
> They rose to a passionate renewal,
> And I must serve their freedoms with my own.

The last line here moves into freedom provided by formal metricality (iambic pentameter) following after the slowing mixture of accentual and durational movement.

And in the end, a place in the poem itself, since one cannot be alive and not be somewhere. OK, a place, but one existing in a sense of community, and because of such existence, some gladness, and a grateful rejoicing. Nor is it always wrong for certainty to engross diffidence and hesitation. Additionally, though I can't say where it occurs, there is mirth of a sort, which shows up because this gladness defies the activity of destruction endemic, perhaps intrinsic, to being human.

INTRODUCTION
Anthony Rudolf

Some readers will want to read only the poems and translations. But scattered through the notes and essays can be found intimations of the man who lived, and, in a fragmentary way, an early assessment of specific aspects of his achievement. The primary task of the editors, though, has been "editorial" rather than "literary critical": we have tried to make it possible for readers to form their own judgment about a body of work that is singular in its ethno-cultural/religious matrix – Judaeo-Scottish. As he wrote in a letter to John Rety: "My real language is probably Scots-Yiddish."

The body of work emanating from the matrix contains poems which time and again project a true voice of feeling mediated by a searching and fastidious intellect. The best poems bear re-reading many times and will survive, because poet and poems are the real thing, transcending the local history of the man's mortal life to speak and sing to readers of all backgrounds. Even as he worries away in his distinctive registers (his use of adjectives, that poetically unfashionable part of speech, merits an entire essay) at his characteristic themes – the exhaustion of Jewish life after the Holocaust, the death of Yiddish, the honouring of his pious Lithuanian-Jewish ancestors, the urban impact of his birthplace Scotland, the English landscape, Jerusalem – Jacobs speaks directly to the reader, as an I to a thou, shaking the hand of the other.

Professionally or vocationally speaking, the poet was known as Arthur Jacobs until some time in the early sixties. He began signing his own work as Arthur C. Jacobs at the beginning of a three year stay in Israel. The 'C' stands for Chaim ("life" in Hebrew). This was a powerful symbolic statement for he was not given this [common enough Jewish] name at birth, but took it on. Later in the sixties Arthur C. Jacobs became and remained A.C.Jacobs. Since we did not want to clutter up the poems with asterisks or key numbers we have put all glosses into a separate notes section, including the known signatures to poems. The signatures were one factor, along with more traditional ones, in helping us establish a provisional chronology in the second section of the book – containing unpublished poems or poems which appeared outside Jacobs' collections – after John Rety had gone through his papers in London and Madrid (see Rety's essay elsewhere in this book). Information from readers, for example a periodical publication which we may have missed and which would place a poem earlier or later or offer a new variant, will be incorporated in any future edition. Following some editors, including the exemplary Oxford University Press *Collected Poems of Basil Bunting*, we felt that most readers would prefer to read the "canon" (see the first section) as published in book form in the poet's lifetime separately from the other poems.

Translation from the Hebrew was an important part of Jacobs' literary work. Anthony Rudolf went through his manuscripts and published work and selected what he felt were the best ones, after discussions with Dr Risa Domb (see elsewhere in the book for an account of this process). As with his original poems, the translations too are differentiated, within the third section, as between the canonical books (one, David Vogel, published in Jacobs' lifetime, the other Ben-Yitzhak, prepared by him but only published after his death) and the unpublished or uncollected work. All bibliographical details concerning poems and translations are presented elsewhere.

On a more personal note, as the publisher of A.C.Jacobs' first book of poems and first book of translations (both in 1976), I remain amazed at the high quality of the unpublished work, including many poems already written at that time. A poem like 'In Early Spring', for example, written in the late fifties when he was not older than twenty-two and published for the first time in late 1995 in *Stand* magazine, how is it possible that this fine poem lay unpublished for decades? Why, indeed, was it not offered to *Stand*, whose editor, Jon Silkin, published an important group of poems by the young Jacobs in 1960? Certainly I do not remember being shown it in 1976. But I am ashamed to say I cannot remember if he presented me with the exact number of poems permitted by the budget or if his perfectionism and obstinacy brooked no discussion.

The section entitled "Other Poems" (see page 173) contains a selection from work that one or other editor felt could have been excluded altogether or, conversely, included in the main body of the book, but was finally negotiated into a separate place. Some holograph poems have proved impenetrable after repeated re-readings and, indeed, may well have only been drafts. Perhaps they will see the light of day in a future publication, along with some of the many poems in early notebooks written when he was less than seventeen. It should also be explained that wherever there were variants in manuscripts we have chosen, following some editors, what we felt was the *best* one (not necessarily the *latest* one, as other editors prefer) and printed the remaining ones in the notes. Readers are free to disagree. Obvious errors of punctuation and spelling have been silently corrected.

I would like to include in this introduction some extracts (occasionally revised) from an obituary I wrote about Arthur in *The Independent*, because they contain a few things it would be appropriate to place on record in this book. But one comment was, happily, quite wrong. I wrote ". . . prolific he was not . . .". That was before John Rety's discovery in the small bedroom in Hendon of the unpublished poems forming much of the second section. We cannot know what Arthur would have made of this book. Some of the poems he would not have wanted to be published, that is certain, but it would have been folly to try to second guess him.

"A.C.Jacobs . . . was a highly individual poet with a distinctive non-metropolitan voice, writing directly out of the experience of his imaginings and the imaginings of his experience . . . He was a shy and retiring man but he often appeared more woebegone and self-deprecating than he really was . . . He could be very funny and was sharply perceptive about fellow writers. Another unexpected trait which became more noticeable over the years was his assertiveness about his work and, above all, his absolutely proper awareness of his own worth and seriousness as a poet."

"I see him now, at poetry readings and publishers' parties, standing quietly with a drink on the margin of the gathering, 'at a slight angle to the universe' (as Forster said of Cavafy), never at the centre of the social whirl. I see him too, as if it was yesterday, at the small party I arranged at home to mark the publication of *The Proper Blessing*. The guests included his fellow Scot, Donald MacRae, the eminent sociologist and occasional poet, who told the gathering that he and his wife often read Jacobs' poems to each other late at night over a proper malt whisky. This best of all possible compliments to a poet delighted Jacobs, it goes without saying."

". . . Sprinkling the bread of affliction with the salt of hope, Jacobs drew on the psychohistorical resources of two minority heritages. Provincial in the best sense – i.e. with a deep awareness of the universal implications of local specificity – he was never parochial. 'Where' . . . is perhaps his most famous poem, and it has been published in several anthologies including the High Holidays prayerbook of the Reform Jewish Movement . . ."

"Born in Glasgow in 1937, Jacobs grew up in a traditional Jewish family and remained very close to his parents throughout his life. In 1951 the family moved to London, where he attended Hasmonean Grammar School. He lived, variously, in Spain (where he died), Israel, Scotland and Italy as well as London. He never married but he had close friendships with several men and women, who appreciated his warmth, who honoured his strangeness, who mitigated his loneliness, who admired his hard-won work which survives him and will survive us. Like his beloved Yiddish-speaking ancestors, Arthur Jacobs awaited redemption in his own Vilna, "a bit east of the Gorbals,/In around the heart".

Postscript:
In an excellent note on A.C.Jacobs published in *The Scottish Review* (1978), along with a selection of poems, George Bruce summarised the Scottish dimension of Jacobs' work as follows:

"In his poem, 'Yiddish Poet', Jacobs writes:

> He loved his language
> Like a woman he had grown old with,
> Whose beauty shone at moments in his memory
> But saw how time had stricken what was his
> And pondered on the truth of his desire

Jacobs' love for the product of community, language, does not blind him to the facts. In Scotland he recognises another community poised between self-realisation and dissipation. A similar melancholy and affectionate tone to that in 'Yiddish Poet' pervades his poem, 'Speech'. There is no yielding to despair, no parading of drama – he still senses the identities of places in his native land, Scotland, and his affection sets him to communicating with delicacy his sense of place. To have achieved a style by which one knows the depth of feeling implicit in the poems 'In Edinburgh Again' and 'Place' is evidence of the genuineness of the man and of his maturity as poet."

Arthur Jacobs
c/o Robert Friend
13 Jabotinsky St.
Jerusalem, Israel

STORY by T. Carmi

When the woman in the fishing-village
Told me of her absent husband
Of the sea that returns every evening to die at her doorstep
I was silent.
I could not say to the shells of her eyes
Your love will return, or
The sea will live again.

(There are days I am unable to find for you
A single word.)

Translated by Arthur Jacobs

CONTENTS **Page**

POEMS PUBLISHED IN BOOK FORM

Note on chronology:

The expanded edition of *The Proper Blessing* (1992) contains a group of seven poems additional to the complete text of *The Proper Blessing* (1976). Two of these poems – 'Region' and 'Breaking' – were reprinted from the group of ten poems published in Jacobs' pamphlet *A Bit of Dialect* (1991): they are included here in the latter sequence. The poems published in *A Bit of Dialect* begin with 'Out' on p.32. The other five poems published in the expanded edition of *The Proper Blessing* begin with 'Uplands' on p.38.

POEM FOR MY GRANDFATHER

On the Anniversary of his Death

Today, a candle in a glass
Burns slowly on the mantelpiece.
Wheesht, the dead are here.

My father, your grey-haired son,
Tastes again the salt, wax prayers
Of your sacred, dying day.

You are a name, holy in his presence,
The last solemn date
In our calendar of death.

Truly a ghost, my father sees, you.
A kind man's regret softens his face.

But for me there is no introduction:
For me you are a light on the mantelpiece,
A half shadow on the wall.

YIDDISH POET

He moved among blocked façades,
And the remains of an old life kept growing
Here and there, for its quaint satisfaction.
In everything the habit of tragedy
Had framed his saddened view.
Sometimes he could not trust himself to speak
For fear of weeping.

He loved his language
Like a woman he had grown old with,
Whose beauty shone at moments in his memory
But saw how time had stricken what was his
And pondered on the truth of his desire.

And he could not remember his own poems
Yet hoped something would live of them,
The scent perhaps, or a sudden particular cry
Made in a night he summed up suffering.

At the end he wrote always of death
As if it was his meaning all along,
And what he hoped from life was not perfection
But difficult glints of certainty.

For a man was this one intimate with sorrow,
His dreams led nowhere – yet alive he sang.

ISAAC

It was my father forced him into the desert –
My father, the patriarch, fearing for my inheritance,
And my mother, jealous of the strength of a concubine's child.

And I vaguely remember the mocking, knowing boy
Who played his secret games around our tents
And crept in at night to his mother the slave woman's pillow.

He could do marvellous things: whistle wild songs,
Climb trees I couldn't, find unknown caves and streams;
His exploits were legend among our lesser household.

But there was that day my father, a man perplexed,
Rejected his furtively proud, unorthodox son:
His God wanted me and my father always listened.

I hear now my brother is chief of a tribe in the desert;
He lives by conquest and has many enemies.
His children plot and starve when he is defeated.

I hear rumours he dreams of marching against me
To seize his inheritance. What shall I do against God and my
father?
I, too, believe in the destiny of my children.

I, too, have suffered, perhaps more than he:
I have had a sacrificial knife laid at my throat.
These lands are a small exchange for that terrifying moment.

I would like to help my brother, but he is still proud.
There will be no discussion of peace between us;
And our father, the old God-fearing man, has been dead many
years.

BEFORE THERE WAS . . .

'Before there was fighting, the road ran south
Through desert to the sea, but when it ended
The frontier cut across, and we built
Another road across it, for direction
And property had altered.'

The old road lay like a severed arm
Grown used to its lack of blood.

Then we climbed higher round the bends
Of ownership the war had left. He pointed
To a tower the shells had chopped into.
'In that tower a bell hung, and two of our men
Were positioned under it. One shell
Brought the bell down, and they were trapped
And killed below.'

Did he say their bodies, or what was left
Of them, still lay under the wrecked iron,
Or did I not follow his words?

At any rate,
For their deaths, a silence passed through us,
All of us held by the sleeping posture of a war.

BEFORE THE TRIAL OF EICHMANN

The cells of that man's brain are divided among us.
Some have its symbols in blue burned into their arms,
Some have a vacancy they will not ever explore
And others see images of cold, dark shadows
That come screaming after them to beg for a pity
That will never be wholly given.

In all of us the bits of brain cry out, cry
For a whole meaning, cry for a design of the machines
We said were human.

We have found no meaning,
And many fragments we cannot ever recover.

But the brain in us cries, the mind invades our mind,
Crying that we should confront the strange, empty cells.
We should take fragments and give them meaning
For the sake of those who died without meaning.

To us this seems human, to judge
For the sake of those who were denied judgement,

To meet, with the fragments crying in us, a cluster
Of empty cells.

LINES

I wrote some lines describing you
As though I had brought
                                        a kind of clarity
To bear on your experience,
As though something, in verse,
Of what you cannot say
                                      was made
Articulate.
                It is a helplessness
Of my own that stares up from the page.
The phrases that were meant
To draw and plead for you
Only dissect,
                    make you more a stranger,
Trap.
         Not everything
                                 is grist for poetry,
Not observation
                          made in place of care.

PRIME OF A STATESMAN

Whatever his real gifts,
                                        whatever
Lonely dramas to match the time's need
He enacted,
                        the leader lives in adulation
Now.
        The party press is warmed
By the mere thought of him,

The opposition are disgruntled
But lie meshed in his legend,

The people are convinced
They cannot do without him

                        And he goes
Bible-quoting,
                            buoyant on history,
So that it seems that government
Is a gift
            for fluent rhetoric.

TASTE

Often we've sat
With brandy, and drunk in Yiddish
Folk-songs, and talked of the wealth
Of material that must lie buried
In unsearched libraries, in mouldering
Collections.
I've felt in touch with
Matters of childhood, and thought my broken
Learning redeemed in the wash of origins.

(Why not these songs also?)

But the only record I found
To commemorate those evenings
Played sentimental tunes.
The schmaltz of its arrangements
Fell horribly.

To savour inheritance is not enough.

JERUSALEM

The town lies in its warm, blue evening,
I can feel the sleep of its easy stones.
There is a small white moon intoning
Put history by: call in your soul.

The dark, quiet streets, untense and shining,
Rock in their comfortable sounds.
The fury of martyred vision murmurs
Put grieving by: call in your soul,

The passion of these small, bare hills crying
On the last grief of Europe washed in them,
On fabulous, split energies shaping
Put searching by: call in your soul.

TEL AVIV 3.30 AM

At three-thirty there is no-one on the streets
Except a few taxi-drivers lounging in
The settled night.
                                        Just out of sight
The dark sea is bashing its meaningless
Shape against the switched out promenade.

The blocks and blocks of flats and offices
Are smoothly silent.
                                        It is all nearly
As brushed and quiet as in Jerusalem

Though here the moon does not hang
Religiously above the sleeping plaster.

These dense and suddenly set down forms
Are the bright shell an unusual courage
Built, a singular innocence fetched up
On unpromising sand.

                                        It is a city
Like any other now, crowded with commerce,
Dazzled by the glare of brutal public signs.
Its faces shift on fashionable tides.

Yet the name still holds a legend
Peopled by the pride of a rebirth.

There is a quick deft brightness
Lingers on the emptied streets,
And its seventy languages
Merge towards the pacing dawn.

SILHOUETTE

She keeps harsh memories of growing up
And twists severely words
to describe her
Northern background,
remembers
Awkwardly her isolation,
too soft
Against her people's weakness.
For this,
She aims at hard images,
summons
A garish pride to stifle
Feelings of lost grace,
yet does not see
How tenderness remains,
the woman she's grown to
Out of the girl's clenched dreams.

PAINTING

The Jew, in the painting by Chagall,
                                        praying.
Armoured in objects of his holiness
He can speak out blessing.
In his dark surroundings
The white *tallis* enfolds him
Like the tent of his piety,
But one edge of it ends,
                        jaggedly,
Near the thongs of the *tefilin*
On his arm.

Under the black box on his forehead
His face burns, sombre, lucid,
But some of it retreats.

The anxiety clenched in it
Mingles with something
Almost a grin.

He sits against darkness
Curling into light.

He is a man
Who bears the weight of his own experience,

What he utters
Will touch
The depths of survival.

GOLDERS GREEN ADDRESS

The place is bland,
trim as any comfortable
Suburb in England,
with all the withdrawn look
Of these neat, affluent times,
but if you looked closely,
Carefully scrutinized,
at times you would see
Small symptoms of alienation
among its well-fed residents.
Candles on Friday,
a beard or two, an occasional
Joke in Yiddish,
but nothing too much,
You understand,
to alarm or remind
Of what there is to be alarmed by
Or be remembered.
You should not imagine
Anyone in the poised main road
would accost
You to blurt out
what has come to pass,
And you need hardly fear
an over-quizzical look,
Or a misplaced gesture.
Though, as I say,
There are one or two signs
of otherness.
Still, don't worry.
They scarcely jar.

MR MARKSON

That old man who came to teach me then
Has blended with many.
                                        I can hardly remember now
Just what he looked like,
                                        except his black hat,
Yellowish stained beard, and shoulders hunched.
His accent too evades me
                                        except that it was broken
Like my grandmother's.

A dark, grey, distant, forgettable man,
Yet three times a week at the dining-room table
He would point to the curling Hebrew script
And pour into me all it said about Creation,
The fall of Adam, and the faith of Abraham.

There was a piety,
                                and something more I couldn't
Understand in all that legend and recital:
A yearning in the old man's broken voice.

GRANDMOTHER

Before she died, my grandmother lay all white
In a bed at the far end of a grim ward,
Cut off from the pieties of ninety years.
                                                                        It was
As though, somehow, the girl she had far away been
Was found again,
                                  chattering in Yiddish,
Babbling in a world her orthodoxy kept hidden
All her days.

                        Her God tormented her
Till, 'Nem tzu mine neshomme,' she cried – 'Take
Away my soul',
                              but the pain went on,
Exhausting the patience of doctors and nurses
Who could not bear one pious old woman's
Plight,
            who could not know the dignities
Racked in her drab body,
                                            or how she was crying.
She died
              through the terrors of a world
That gave no answers
                                        to what she cried.

FESTA

Today they say was the feast
Of *Corpus Domini*
                    And coming round
By the cathedral, I blundered
Into the vast crowds gathered
To watch the spectacle.
                          There were
Slow drum taps, and then the
Banners came, swaying out of
The great doors, and round the square,
Followed by God's agony carved
On a little cross of sticks.
                           An anthem
Struck up through the well-placed
Loudspeakers, and someone prayed
In a level, finely pitched voice
For the poor, the prisoners, the sick
And unemployed.
                    The crowd answered
Ascoltaci,
          And a white canopy,
Like a *chuppah*, came billowing round.

I saw many near me duck and
Cross themselves in their devotion.

                                   It was
Soaring and death, on the square
Of San Giovanni, a glimpse at a
Beautiful ceremony.
                      I lit a cigarette,
Thoughtfully, and walked away.

REMOTE ISLAND

There was that lonely island in the North,
Best for the birds, but a few people lived there
In small and difficult crofts.
                                        There was a hill
That rose slowly on one side of it, and across the top
Were the ruins of a war-time establishment.
                                                            Huge
Water-tanks rusted there, and tough generators
Lay in derelict silence, crumbling.
                                                Strong walls had just
A few gaps in them, but broken fences swayed over
The hillside.
                It was like the remains
Of a previous civilisation on the island,
Though it was twenty years or so ago, the place
Was built.
              And strolling through it you could see
How expertly the war had raised it up,
And just as quickly had dismantled it,

Leaving the island, still depopulating,
In its old remoteness, at the edge of things.

WRITING

Your last writing covered pages
With huge, thick, sprawling shapes
As though fiercely you were trying to staunch
Some great wound, and as if
Ink were blood.
                    The furious loops
Of the letters tell nothing,
                              except that
Ink or blood was pouring out of you
Over paper that didn't hold.

TRAVELLING ABROAD

Documents, scrutinies, barriers,
Everywhere I pass through them,
It seems, without difficulty.
Nothing jars, nothing slips out of place,
Authority is satisfied by my credentials.

Really, it must represent some peak
Of achievement, from a Jewish
Point of view, that is.
                         What a time
It's taken to bring me
To this sort of freedom,
What tolls have been paid
To let me come
                    to this kind
Of passage.

I can appreciate it,
believe me,
I can appreciate.

But I find myself wondering,
As I sit at this café table
over
A good glass of beer,
Why I don't feel something more
like gratitude,
Why there's some form of acceptance
I don't grasp.

VISITING

It was fine visiting you in Cambridge.
I could see the soft misty elegance
Of that famous town in late November,
And who wouldn't recall a few at least
Of the great names harboured there.
We sat
In a bright hall opposite your college
and listened
To an excitingly renowned American poet
Nervously probing his packed, tense lines.
You deserve
All that the place can offer you,
all that mysterious learning
In store there.
I was thinking that, as I walked
Back to the station, between the gentle buildings,
And passed a gang of youngsters, jeering
at a Japanese couple.

WHERE

I find it is Yom Kippur,
and here I am
Down by the river
in late afternoon.
There is a poem
I have read
In several versions
about the Jewish writer
Who doesn't fast, who
doesn't go to synagogue
On Yom Kippur,
the day of atonement,
And here is my construction
of that poem.
Here am I,
on the embankment
Staring at the river,
while the lights
Are coming up,
signifying darkness, the end of the fast,
Though it's not over yet,
and the congregations
Are still gathered
in the synagogues,
Praying, *slach lonu, m'chal lonu,*
forgive us, pardon us,
We have sinned,
we deserve punishment,
We are like clay
in the hands of the great Potter,
Who has shaped us all,
even, you could say, me

Here by the river,
watching the water
And the rubbish
drifting on the water,
Imagining what is
swaying in under the bridges,
Is something of exile,
formless but perceptible,
Bringing in the names
of pious cities,
Vilna and Minsk and Vitebsk
(my own ancestral names)
And vanished communities,
behind curtains
Of forgetfulness,
and ordinary human change,
Praying communities
on Yom Kippur and other days
Clinging to and turning from
that which I cling to
And turn from,
if you like, the covenant
That keeps me fasting,
but not in synagogue
Today, Yom Kippur.
I go into the gardens,
Sit down on a bench,
read my newspaper
And wait
for the first star.

DETERRENTS

The road began in a dismal bus station
In the centre of Glasgow, and ran through
Famous slums soon into green countryside.

It was beautiful: this is what the songs
Praise, what Scottish exiles drift to
In that well-known *heimweh*. The air

Was raw and fresh, and the waters
Of the lochs really like glass. I could
Drive for years through such countryside.

It's worth defending, you would say,
And sure enough there are sharp warning notices
Beside some lochs, provided by the Ministry

Of Defence, to all citizens to stay clear
Of the torpedoes, I think it was torpedoes,
They shoot off from time to time. Ah well,

They need security, such splendid scenes,
But I must say, seeing the notices, and thinking
Of those weapons, I felt anything but secure.

BOOKSELLERS

It hasn't taken long for even the street to go.
That crowded little street last time I saw it
Was smashed up and naked. Why should I mourn
Except for that bookseller who hoarded his volumes
There in a dark little shop, holy books and profane,
A transient collection brought over from the Continent
When such books were being torn and burnt, by decree?
Huge volumes of Talmud, small volumes of poetry,
Grammar and philosophy, guides for the perplexed,
The fruits of exile carefully reassembled
In another kind of ghetto.
                                        After he died, I saw
His shop abandoned, ruined, opened to the illiterate air.
It had suffered a fire, and the burnt, soused collection
Lost touch with its identity.
                                        Through the charred mess
I saw a fine copy of the stories of Mendele,
Writer of Yiddish, who called himself 'the Bookseller'.

SOUND

In a rough, windy night
I have been listening
To the movements of the wind
And forming a kind of poem
Without knowing its language.

Ruach, I say, using
The old biblical word
For the wind, the breath
Or spirit of God
Moving after creation.

But nothing follows:
No other words
Cross the darkness outside.
There is only *ruach*,
The word for the sound of the wind.

AWARENESS

It's Princes Street at festival time.
In the bandstand in the gardens a concert
Is just finishing. God save the Queen.
Two rather bedraggled girls are passing
And, catching the tune, one suddenly asks
The other in good, natural Doric
If she knows that song is anti-Scottish,
Though she can't remember exactly what
It says about us. God save the Queen.

RULING

'Without the Law,'
Shouted the lawman,
'You will be cudgelled
And abused by
Nameless bullyboys.
All kinds of dreadful
Unforeseen, chaotic things
Will happen to you,
And you won't like it,'
He cried, waving
His enormous club.

THREE POEMS ABOUT DEATH

From the Hebrew of Moses Ibn Ezra
Lived and Died in Spain, 11th - 12th century

1

A man should remember, from time to time,
That he is occupied with death,
That he is taken a little further
On a journey every day
Though he thinks he is at rest,
Like a ship's passenger lounging on deck,
Being carried on by the wings of the wind.

2

I was stirred to visit the resting place
Of my parents and all my true friends.
I questioned them, but they neither heard
Nor answered me. Have even, I asked,
My own mother and father betrayed me?
Without speaking they called to me
And showed me my own place beside them.

3

There are graves remaining from long ago
In which men sleep out eternity.
There is neither envy nor hatred,
Love nor malice there, and looking
Over them I could not separate
Who was slave and who was master.

ANTIQUITY

It is only an old metal pot
With a half-intelligible Hebrew inscription
Round its middle.
                                        No one knows
What it could have been used for.
It was found in an English river
In the seventeenth century.
                                                        It is medieval,
And stands today in a glass case
In a museum.
                              I stare at it,
Wondering.
                              Perhaps its message
Is meant for me.

PESSIMISTIC NOTE

The times are getting sour:
Scapegoats are being looked for.
Where do they go looking for them?
Where have they looked before?

IMMIGRATION

1

It wasn't easy getting out of the Tsar's Russia.
They had to bribe and lie.

And it was terrible on the ship.
They couldn't go up deck,
Someone stole all their luggage,
And the children were sick with fever.

Still, she came through it, my young grandmother,
And travelled to Manchester,
Where my grandfather was waiting, with a new language,
In Cheetham Hill.

2

Really, they'd wanted to reach America,
But never saved enough for the tickets,
Or perhaps it was just that their hearts were in the east,
And they could go no further west.

However it was, when Hitler went hunting,
We found that luckily
They had come far enough.

THE HUNDRED PIPERS

Dumbfoundered the English they saw, they saw,
Dumbfoundered they heard the blaw, the blaw,
Dumbfoundered they a' ran awa', awa'

I remember how the teacher's voice crowed
As she taught us that song. How we enjoyed it!
I still do, this battle song of my native country.

Looking back,
I wonder what wars she was preparing us for,
That ancient miss.

RETURN

After a long time in the desert
What is it that brings back poetry
Like water to the Negev?

I don't know. Not virtue
Or debauchery, or any special hardship
Or sudden love.

I'd better, anyhow,
Make the most of it,
And say the proper blessing
For such occasions.

OUT

All the poems not collected,
That are left lying in drawers
Among dying papers, or go roaming
On pages one can't recall,
Which of them really exist
And which are imagined?

When sortings take place they glow
And gnaw.

There should be some ceremony
Like *Kol Nidrei*, the solemn cancellation
Of all vows unaccomplished,
For these untended poems.

Whatever one owes them ought
To be erased.

REGION

On this side down through the trees
You come to the haugh, and the river
Flowing clearly over its stones.
                                        The field
Across it leads up to the main road,
Duly numbered, signposted and flat.

And on the other side, if you go up
Alongside the burn, into the fields, you come
To a ridge where clumps of heather cling
And you can look down past the curving
Of the hills into the next valley.

                                        Beyond those
More hills bulge up to the sky.
                                        There are
Few buildings, byres mostly, or low cottages
In the distance.
                        On maps it is
All named, this place, accounted for.

But to me looking over it now
Towards the sunset
                        it is a nameless country
That could be mine.

FROST

The trees stand apart and fragile.
The fields offer themselves with whiteness.
There is shrivelling everywhere:
Winter's exposures have begun.

SPEECH

Out here in the hills you get
Quite a bit of dialect,
                                        more than many
People would imagine.
                                          It's had a way
Of surviving, breaking out, whatever
Gentility may say,
                                   beyond where education
Leads.
        I have an ear for it,
Scots or Yiddish,
                                   raw expression
                                                      that
No one's quite sure
                                      how to handle.

PLACE

'Where do you come from?'
'Glasgow.'
'What part?'
'Vilna.'
'Where the heck's that?'
'A bit east of the Gorbals,
In around the heart.'

MOVEMENT

The girls wore white blouses
And navy blue skirts.
We wore our school caps –
It was the religious youth movement.

We learned simple songs in Hebrew,
Danced the *hora*, heard stories of heroism.
We went scouting in lanes and fields
Behind the synagogue.

It was Glasgow, the dark time
After the war.
Rosa and Sonia and those others
Whose names I don't remember

What became of them,
Our leaders, ripening?
Did they go and settle and bear soldiers
In the promised land?

PLEASE NOTE

I've never claimed great, accurate knowledge:
I've always lived in doubt,
But I haven't been quite as ignorant
As authorities have made out.

SOL

'See the sun redden towards evening'

Near Malaga, I see the sun
Reddening, yellowing into the blue sea
And think of Shlomo ibn Gabirol,
Malagueñan, who wrote that line.

And this afternoon I drank a cup
Of sweet wine in a hidden square
Where Lorca drank and is remembered,

It is the time of *El Cambio*,
Changing. The Moors are gone,
The Catholic realm is gone,
The heady dictatorships are dregs.

The other end of the Mediterranean,
Where I have also been, fumes.

The poems sing their lusts, their elegies.

Córdoba, Granada, sierras, exile.

Old passions cry in measured times.

Torre del Mar, January 1988

BREAKING

A bad season. War broken out
And round about more personal fears.

In this I am supposed to look
For images, to touch rhythms, to speak.

I have no binding sounds,
No singing linkages,

Can only turn and turn and listen
For some calm to come.

PRIVATE

Oh, well, look,
This is a poem for you.
You know who I mean.

I'm not going to say anything
About our comings and goings.

If anyone else
Wants to butt in
They can try
But I'm not going to say anything.

This is just for you.
You know who I mean.

UPLANDS

I climb the hills
And it is all my life
I'm looking down on,

Acres and acres
Swinging there in the valley.

I never realised
They could be so far away.

WORK

'What do you do?'
'Translate.'
'Oh? What language do you
Translate from?'
'Hebrew.'
A sudden, adjusting silence
And then? And then?

LOOK

Here's a drunk man,
Some kind, he says, of academic,
A right man of feeling,
Sneering at me, in the Abbotsford,
Scatologically, for being a poet.

What's he scared of?

Does he think I'll blow the whistle
On his cultivated thistle?

LEARNING

I too was a student of those things,
The texts and commentaries.
My readers know all this,
My references.

And after all that (knowledge buried
Like damaged scrolls of the Torah)
What of it?

It's all asking.
                    Though I've forgotten much
Of the debate and ritual,
The rhythms of learning,
It's still in me to ask and ask.

ITZIG MANGER BROWSES THROUGH THE PAPERS IN PARADISE

Manger sits in *Gan Eden*
Drinking a glass of tea.
The 'Heavenly Literary Supplement',
In Yiddish, is on his knee.

He sees a review of his poems,
The finest he's ever read.
A *mechayye*, he says, to be written about
This way after I'm dead.

He looks to see who wrote it,
This critical masterpiece.
Aha, it was *Dovid Hamelech*!
Wonders will never cease.

And then he sees a translation
Of a poem written by me.
A.C.Jacobs, he murmurs,
Now who on earth could he be?

He reads it through without stopping:
Oy, is this a poem, says he.
It's the best I've read in ages –
I mean that literally.

Then he turns to Kafka,
Asks, Franz, have you seen this?
Tell Heine and Yehuda Halevi
Here's something they shouldn't miss.

We must get his work included
In God's Oxford anthology,
And tell the Angel Gabriel
To send him a generous fee.

POEMS UNCOLLECTED IN BOOK FORM/ UNPUBLISHED POEMS

In provisional chronological order

OY

Funny exclamation
Almost as if it were born in another climate
Driven out from mouths by a foreign wind.

Yet its dirty liquid sorrow
Wails in our streets and ruins our houses
As if the very walls had sinned.

And a brick conspiracy
Keeps the sound for eternal sighing
Though the gods who heard it only grinned.

HYDROGEN-BOMB TEST

Somewhere, near the crouching islands of Japan,
Cupped death spilt out over the ocean,
And no-one died.

And no-one knew what insane phoenix
Climbed to the sun from the bits in the water,
Or where it landed.

One afternoon a child went ordinarily mad,
And several warned and wiser people wondered
If somehow it was bitten by the bird.

May 15 1957

A JEW IN GLASGOW

Yesterday I walked all morning
In the decayed ghetto of the fierce Gorbals.
In Hospital Street, where my father was born
I saw Odessa leaning out to sea
And all the old cities of Lithuania
With grimy curtains drawn across their dreams.

A girl no older than myself
Looked at me, with drug bitten eyes
And Celtic prostitution in her heart.

There are strange clans who fight around these walls
With warcries in their throats
That deserve no glory.

Across the oily waters of the river,
Poorly designed for suicide,
I watched the unhappy movement of a great city
And I knew that within its hungry streets
Move lives more lonely than our own.

POEM FOR INNOCENT VICTIMS OF WAR

You did not die for me
Or love or desperation.
No-one chipped your names
On plaques on peaceful blocks of stone.
You are just the useless dead
Who mock our daily sin of passion,
Climb through our heads in cold, slow silence.

When you were people
We could have loved you,
Found out your names
And brought you presents.
We could have walked around with your response.

Or even if you chose to die
We might have understood your longing
And written down your utmost fear.

Now, though, you have got beyond our feelings,
And we can never almost follow
To learn your last shared and perfect secret.

ABRAHAM

Long ago the eviction came from God
And he turned towards a dedicated West
Not fleeing, but looking for a land
Bound in strange dreams and blessings.
And not like the prophets' in their nights
Of visions, poems in God's illumination,
His notice came: but in the clear day
In the ancestral town of Ur
His mind flashed with a message.

History never marked his journey with
A coloured line on maps of time.
Yet in the scrawled legends he is
To be found, the stranger in a strange land.
His settlement left no altars, temples,
Palaces to guide his children round,
Only a well or field or cave he dug
Or bought or sowed. He rose early and
Sacrificed, or nearly did, his son. We weep

For this father and his God, and for ourselves
We make his journey thrice a day.

LANGSIDE

The grey cloak of the city
Loosens on this hill.
The summit, half proud, inhales
The air of battle,
And more ashamed sinks into memory.

A tall queen, sad and ghostly,
Sometimes mounts the wind
To her dearly tragic end,
But no echoes fall
On the street's formality of traffic.

This hill holds her spirit
Above the unmoved town
Of this strange slow dying land:
Too proud to keep a queen,
Too meek to serve its own wisdom.

HAMPSTEAD HEATH: BANK HOLIDAY

Tumbling around my head the people go
With the dust kicked into the hot air
A sullen mist to the inquiring sun.
Hurling themselves from stone corners
Into this high patch of din and uncaught strife
Voices whirling through cheap rhythms
Are even cheaper; and meeting here are unreal
Worlds of happiness tapering into a thin
Arena of careless sense, while demon fear
Climbs into the blue sky and vanishes.
One afternoon has bought the shrill sensation
Of a dirty year.

And then returned to my quiet home
Thought resumes its usual sphere
And in the silent night I wonder:
How much life did I buy at the fair?

THE VICTIM

Her children must have changed for Golders Green
Or Richmond, and left her to be a dignified scavenger
Among the incredible junk of Whitechapel.

Too fat to be a crone,
And yet fearful to children
She trundles home the picked outcast tatters
She will make into odd garments.

Today, while she shifts her scraps
Up the close to the unseen locality
Of her fierce transformations,
She shouts with her face tilted
To the top of the building

And, not as the mad are supposed to be,
She is coherent,
And doesn't mutter:
Yet pedestrians smile, and drivers wink at their companions.

'Hitler sent people to gas-chambers',
She tells her miraculous, sympathetic audience,
'And those villains took my machine'.

The single profitable instrument among her furniture
Is gone, and when her supporting monologue is over
She will climb the stairs
And sit calling on God to amend the future.

It is useless to tell her the state gives pensions
To those whom fate has disemployed.
How can you help someone plagued by Hitlers?
What can you do with a proud unmarriageable widow?

SOVEREIGN PENNY

1

My grandfather, the benevolent head
On a penny, pressed in my scraped fist
Will not be twisted across
His round flat smiling world.

2

He crouches away from awkward holes
That have lost me many coins
Down in the hot hell of my pocket,
He won't suffocate.

3

This infinite well-wisher
Falls untouched through the steel
Throats of slot machines
Back into my bent hand.

4

Thrown to the sun, he spins
His grin back to the dust
And waits obtrusive
For me to pick him up.

5

I know what he wants:
To be a proud charm on a string round my neck.
When I tug at him for luck or breath
I'll choke.

THE INFINITE SCALE

The books and scrolls of our suffering
Outweigh the huge stone image of our God
And elegies rise, with their sickness, in our throats
More surely than the wrapped, counted words of prayer.

It is terrible to walk under these mountains of suffering
For ties intrude outside the power of words.
When I suggest my love's least comfortable need
The round figure is formed of the destroyed.

I want to measure my wounds by those who have not gone
        so far in agonies,
To have a less knowledgeable conscience.
But such standards are not for me to make:
To be told, the massive guilt remains.

POEM FOR JOHN KNOX

A goading, rigid puritan,
You were most of the landscape.

And my grandfather, without formal recognition,
Must have met you many times.

He would have seen his children
Chipped and shaped by the harsh rigour of your words.

And wondered at the smell of debate
You spread among the trespassing city:

Though his dream of final revealed redemption
Could never be obliterated,
But flourished more in this jealous, acid soil.

You, too, would have made a garden here,
Though with mostly home-grown seed:
And certainly your roots have squirmed and stretched
And stiffened under the lashed earth.

I, sinning against my grandfather's messiah,
And the tang of restraint you imposed on my neighbours,
Remember and am consoled
By burd Helen and the loves of Robert Burns.

VERSES OF ANXIETY

Granny, look up from your prayer book:
Use your eyes, that cannot read
The words that spark across continents,
To discover the insane, monstrous way of the world.

I tell you they are going to blow us all to bits:
America, the huge land of potential miracles
You in your exile never got as far as,
And the cold burst motherland of Russia
Lost somewhere in your obscure nightmare.

Don't you understand? it is no persecution.
They are talking of this at reputable conferences.
It is not all part of the usual blood lust;
We shall none of us suffer the glory of martyrdom.

And anyway, they have long ago classified your God
Among the more puerile myths of mankind.
They have proved the world is not flat and the sky is not heaven,
It is thought that few sinners are easily condemned.

Though maybe you are right to repeat prayer after prayer,
To have built a confident tower of words,
For when you join your unlimited company of the dead
You can't be sure you'll be correctly mourned.

POEM IN MEMORY OF ALL THE JEWISH GIRLS
who were made prostitutes for German soldiers and then suffered the ultimate martyrdom

I

You, who walk under the lights of London,
Who have buried your dead in sacred graveyards,
Come with me: I will show you my sister.

Leave your bright, high strung advertisements
Tear up your theatre tickets
And come through my falling silence.

II

"Behold, thou art fair, my sister, my bride,"
In the very first leap of your love.

She dreamed early of love
And her body grew slowly
To meet its sharp fulfilment.
Truly she tended a soul.

To her, knowledge would come
Gently, with soft tears.
Her smiles would touch the world like dew.

But one morning the world changed.
Screaming and fire burst out
And ran across fields and houses.
Men moved with purpose
To an end called Death.

At first she shared the terror
Dancing in the blood of all
Till suddenly it swooped
And stopped, silent beside her.

A knock at the door at night
And she was caught, like a bird.
She did not beat against her fate.

III

My sister is dumb in the hands of her spoilers.
The eyes of my bride stare at those who will rape her.

Her clothes lie at her feet. She is naked,
In the daytime. Her flesh is marked
With fire, for she is a useful animal.

They will teach her the ritual of her dream.

See, my bride, your lover comes.
His fatherland is that lust in his eyes.
Be proud and do not be afraid:
You are a barren daughter of Zion.

Do not cry out for the princes of your people;
A German soldier wants your body;
Your soul is thrown out into the wilderness.

At last, what was my sister broke
When she was past despair.
They led her to the front of her sisters
In her last nakedness
That had abandoned any shame
And flogged out every cry

She had before refused.

Then they flung her dead stained body
Into a furnace.
The pitying flames ate up her wounds.

IV

We have prayers for the dead.
We have words for the living:
But nothing will tell of this, my sister's death.

She, without a face,
Is more than all the dark women of Solomon,
Her weeping hurts more than Rachel's,
Samson's strength could not avenge her.

V

You, who have come with me,
Look at my sister in her nakedness.
Gaze at the young breasts of my bride.

Is she not dark and comely?
See why I cry in my cold bed.

Go back, now, go back
And leave me in this place
Till I have found my sister's bones.
(Twelve years' weeds are mingled in their shame).

Take back with you,
Back to your troubled cities,
Its many names:
Auschwitz, Belsen, Buchenwald,
Theresienstadt, Dachau,
Treblinka . . .

NEVER YOU

It could not have been you I loved
When the big tree by your window
Lent the room those feasts of blossom.

It could not be you
For whom I looked for words
To call up your thin dark beauty
From our moderated pain.

And it wasn't you
Who understood more than was needed,

For your words are small and stupid,
Your hard, clothed body is obscene.
Keep away from me for ever:
You are all I hate.

OLD LADY

Her age became her, and when she talked
Of beauty it was what she most understood
Being one relic of a passing form
That had not turned sagged and crude
But rested in the sleek turning of her hair,
The masterly placing of hands, and the sound
Of her voice reading her small poems
In a warm spring night over the park.
One did not criticise her words but calmly
Listened, and watched her skilled movements.

THROUGH THE DARK HOUSE . . .

Through the dark house a man
Cries in his sleep. I am
Downstairs writing a poem.

His voice curls through night
Like a yellow ghost, though he
Is roped to that dream he dies in.

Horror of his helplessness
Stills what is already still.
My fierce, clawed voice stops.

ON A TRIP TO YORK

In 1190 there was a massacre of the Jews at York.

In the narrow, crowded streets
Of this cold northern town
I remember the elegies for the besieged martyrs
Of nearly eight hundred years ago.

And in the Minster, where
The good archbishops gently smile in stone,
I want to scream in Hebrew
Up the great square tower
And dance on the placid flagstones
Kicking at the scrupulous shock
For the death of one improbable Jew.

But I stand and watch the choirboys, two by two,
In red and white, marching to evensong,

And think: The dead of York and Kiev and Warsaw
Lie in no ghetto in the heart.

Our words to mourn them storm the common air
When they are fierce and bleak and fact.

ALIEN POEM

I was born in a strange land.
Though I never invoked strangeness
The houses' grey walls
Of the town that was chosen
Kept back secrets, because of my lateness.

And though my father remembered
Other towns with trams and trees and silence
Their secrets, too
Would not be shared
With vagabonds, however respectable.

Strangers never grow into cities,
And their children encumbered with memories
Are clumsy, and afraid
They miss too much.
Sometimes, the strangeness is itself a promise.

THE ANARCHIST

He saw the world was wrong:
Power shaped in ignorant vessels,
And knew he had to break them
For his own way to claim the sun.

So climbing from his cellar
He hacked in daylight at the state,
And some gods fell cracked open.
Their power ran seething round the sky,

But cooled in a few shallow pots.
He, in his dungeon, waiting for hemlock,
Renounced all abstractions,
And savoured the ease that could have made him king.

TOWARDS A GRIEF

Sometimes a poem is a desecration of grief,
(When our brave detachment from the act of love
Turns to a vicious instrument that rips
A hard and human passion to acceptable phrases).

I say now only that the eyes of her I love
Are swollen, and at times her voice trembles.
My knowledge of what she feels turns elsewhere,
These lines have nothing for either of us.

YOU

You creep like a hungry animal
Up to all my feasts of words,
And though you are always silent
I am troubled by your presence.

A guest whose need is not made known
Should want no sustenance
But you bring justice with your silence
And I must make provision

Since I have asked you once to stay
And you never replied, but waited
As if there were more formalities.
Speak, just, and tell me what I have omitted.

POEM TO A SICK WOMAN

You never learned that suffering was an art:
How to convey the pain that roamed the acres
Of your hurt inside that everyone tried to avoid.
I suffer, you said, *and no one understands.*

Grief, like great love, requires some talent, which we
Mostly do not possess, unhappily imitate;
Being not lesser Christs but passing fools
Whose little martyrdoms are interesting, then bore.

I know you suffer in some bestial way,
Your body's poison rages on your peace,
But for these most you have my awkward sympathy –
The maimed words that stumble when you start to tell.

AGAINST THE IDEOLOGIES

Troubles of vision in those half documented days
Would all resolve in water or spinning fire,
Symbols with fingers pointing the eventual truth,
God's earthly instructions in a heavenly choir;

And my kind, burning reassured and grim,
Descend to threaten and sap the profane
Alliance with false gods, other nations and the devil.
Prophets alone were once accounted sane.

Now I move among people, uneasy, and far from sure
Of divine backing for my proffered words.
Nor are these shaped lilting for entertainment –
I haven't the ear of ancient musical bards.

No, a few parties, some nostalgic journeys north,
The second-hand image of a recent war
Thrust wavering questions at my spiritual self.
I, the groping seer, can't answer, for

The shackled absolutes are smashed, the carriers
Of the Message are madmen in the park.
I affirm man's faith in his lack of prophetic wisdom;
In practice I record his growing in the dark.

A GLOSS ON TALMUD

It is written the soul sits
Thirty days brooding and tormented
Over the deathly fixed flesh of the loved body.

After it sees all kinds of caresses are wasted
And is filled with the horror of the skin's colour
It turns at last and departs to its particular after-life.

We are not told how before resurrection
It will manage to slide back into the shock
Of taking on again the disgusting mould it finally tried to forget.

For we have learned in another place:
On that day their bodies will be resumed by all the dead.
Let's hope each disembodied soul is taught to surmount
Its distaste for this unhappy arrangement.

RECORD OF A WALK HOME

It was a lovely booze-up, and we were
Walking home through the naked midnight streets
Stepping across tramlines like the metal sinews
Of a satisfied city falling into sleep,

When one of us, a medical student, drawled
Of a child as I might speak of a poem
Gone wrong: 'Poor little bastard, got jaundice,
And it's going to die. Nothing to do

But let it.' I stopped sick at the jest
That made a human being serve our drunken
Sentimentality. Then thought: My pity
Orders words to save the growth of life,

But if a car came plunging down this road
And caused an accident, I would stand by
And watch while he fought for the sufferer.

I walked on and caught the others up,
Thinking of either deficiency
That kept our trades apart.

'INTRODUCTION TO A SCOTTISH SEQUENCE'

What called me north I do not know
Entirely. Not a piper on a rock
Dirling hypnotic music through my sky,
Nor lust for whisky washed down with strong ale
Against a foggy background of bare hills,
Nor Raeburn's beauties near ethereal
(With jeans and shorter hairstyles, nowadays)
Made me leave her in the south
Who was cool and English, and the fierce
Jewish discussions of unfathomable hate.

I am no exile from a Celtic mist
Nor wanderer from 'the Northern lights
of Aberdeen'. To me exile is a country,
That has the face of the cities of Europe,
A slum face pocked with treacherous suburbs.

And yet looking down South Portland Street
Towards an old fashioned stretch of the River Clyde
I perceive that what I am after is mostly
Again my grandfather, that man strong in Talmud,
(And I myself in Turriff Street long ago
Was taught the dialogue of ingenious rabbis)
What kept him here for almost fifty years,
That calls, but cannot keep me here, for one?
What gave this place the look of an outpost of exile
To woo the east here in his daily prayers?

His son's son, I cross the river into town
Looking for bejeaned models of Raeburn (or any
Other painter) or listening to neutral music.

The old man's secret rests with him
Behind these stricken stones.

INTERLUDE

"Let Glasgow. . . . "

From a broad window of the Art Gallery
I stare down at the beauty of Kelvingrove.
An attendant, like an imitation gendarme,
Is standing fixedly beside me. I think
In a moment he is going to ask me to leave
For not looking at the pictures.

SUPPLICATION

Lord, from this city I was born in
I cry unto you whom I do not believe in:
(Spinoza and Freud among others saw to that)
Show me in this place in which I started
Where I have gone wrong.

Descend neither in Kirk nor synagogue
Nor university nor pub.

But on a handy summit like Ben Lomond
Make me a new Sinai, and please God
Can we have less of the thou-shalt-not?

PARTY AT DOONFOOT

Across the bay at Ayr the confident holidaymakers
Down from Glasgow for a day's slow paddling duration
Eat up the beach with cries, ice-creams and deck-chairs.
We watch the gulls, and try to ignore the people in our eyes' crowded corner.

The hot sun dries what we lift of ourselves out of the sand,
The scaur's black outline falls unmenacingly into the sea,
And starting to walk over the pools and stone to our deserted bit of water
We have found a kind of completion in our Sunday coastward journey.

After the bathe the scorched cars wait for our impatient drive home
Down to Kilmarnock, and over the rejected, melancholy moors
To supper and the routine dance with its hopelessly familiar faces.

This afternoon we believed we had stolen time:
Now back in the mis-shapen, persistent city
We feel our theft drummed into a slick repetitive rhythm.

POEM

I am a tall talmudic Jew
With a slightly Scots accent.
You are English whom the sun
Never tans, but strokes your white skin.
Between us we lay bare your breasts
And gently my fingers pluck and gently
Your arms enfold.
                              Where afterwards
Sad colours in the sky grow from
I do not know.

A JOKE ACROSS THE NORTH SEA

Watching the neat, vacant firth
Opposite the dull shoulder of Fife coast
I stood at the edge of the sea's doorstep.

One of an island bundle, I heard
The poet Heine calling to Scotland
Across the cold, liberating waves.

Ha, how you would laugh, dead sweet-bitter singer,
To hear one, tugged like you, at the seams of his Jewish coat,
Rise, like me, to try and answer.

THE DEPARTURE

At sunrise we sighted his departure
Halfway up the hillside
And though we knew he would go
Into his own oblivion
As if we had not driven him
Our souls called him back;
But he was among the morning cries
Of the indifferent birds, and the rocks
Moved him into a familiar background.

This scene requires belief
Though not as he demanded
With a cry to the soul and a promise.
We remain among his burning words.

His words burned in the shadow of our existence
As the truth burned in his brain:
All the elements sufficed to wield his truth
Yet the tools were easily divided.

To fashion images of truth
He chose the future, and arranged its scenes
With a single meaning. There was no
Gap a poet leaves.

All this we understand
Though we rejected him.
It is bitter in a corner of our hearts.

Perhaps I should have gathered my doubts
Into an echoing call of return.
Would the city drag my voice
Down from the revealing wind?

It is too late now.
The gods of the city call for worship

And he is gone into his own oblivion.

I CHOOSE NEITHER . . .

I choose neither East nor West,
For I am shaped by the North,
And my history reaches down through old maps
Of Europe, and jumbled alphabets meaning,
'I am for ever. This my Empire stands.'

Only those I seek who say: 'Pain is real,
And not to be put by with a shrug,
Nor exhibited.'
And also: 'Love is more than a gesture' and
'Know what you destroy'.

But those who scrutinize and say:
'You do not fit the pattern of my analysis',
'So many laws are broken here',
'The gods, our teachers, do not like that',
Are those whom I want to avoid, my enemies.

To those who think my choice simple I write:
For these and for want of these
The blood of my relatives and ancestors
Ran down the gutters of empires.

It flows in me like a cold, rough sea.

IN EARLY SPRING

Walking in Hampstead in early Spring,
Where the patches of mud on the Heath
Reminded me of Winter's diseases no sun could get at,
I summoned my verses, such as they were,
To survey their afflictions and measure their promise.

And here in this cool English suburb
There grew in me the sound of all the singers
Who turned my people towards Jerusalem,
Or, hopeless in exile, mourned the loss of fulfilment
And the human errors that warped their love.

The Hebrew ones who clung to the purity
Of that vision that promised them return,
Yehudah Halevi, and Moses Ibn Ezra,
A man of love, whose learning served to make
A perfect poem, and know a bad one by instinct;

And afterwards Bialik who came near to seeing
What those ones in Spain knew only was a dream,
Though he knew too what centuries wound round their hearts
Enclosed his people in futility of words,
And rose and sang them out of stupor.

And also those whose sprawling anguish
Spread out in Yiddish across the grim frontiers,
And saw the tongue they nourished dying
Through what they too had longed for.
And those who in the many tongues of Europe

Were figures of exile, voices of victims,
Men torn by what they did not always know.
The ironic Heine, whose sharp sad lyrics,
Removed from the text-books, did not die
But ruined the Germans' perfect solution;

And tragic Rosenberg, whom a war killed
Before he got his great things into words;
My friend Jon Silkin; and those over the Atlantic
Looking at Europe like a distant curse.
And I hear most the miraculous, broken poems

That were made in the enclosures of insanity
Whose authors heard the chanting of the Inquisition
And smelt the smoke of the crematoria
And knew there was no escape, yet wrote
To show how life is at the verges of humanity.

Their great sound grew, and in that company
I walked past the pond and down the hill,
Aware that nothing was ended. With this Spring
They rose to a passionate renewal,
And I must serve their freedoms with my own.

THE ASTROLOGER

His flat and battered notebook
Is like grey parchment with symbols
Scrawled in its dust out of Babylon.

He will set, for three and sixpence,
Round your magic hour of birth
The stars that in their movements

Tell him the secrets your appearance
Chose for itself. He is no crank,
But a true survival from an ancient

Art that promises trends, not detailed
Incident. Consult him at your peril:
For whether or not his assured vision

Excites the protest of your intellect,
Past and future turn before his gaze,
Mortality lies naked beneath his fingertips.

O, ENGLAND

The artistry of driving trains
Fills me with awe, outward bound
From Bradford (Forster Square) to Leeds (City).
To command a clear track, excluding tunnels,
Requires a keen eye, which I have not,
And a firm hand to brake and speed
Through factories and curving rivers.
O, England, sensed at Apperley Bridge,
What powers control you?
O, England, poised at Newlay and Horsforth,
Whose is your country, greenwood and smoke-stack?
Who, England, like the driver of a diesel,
Sees you in front of him, virgin and laden
With grim encroachments?

'MY FATHERS PLANNED ME'

My fathers planned me with their prayers
And gave me their coded, ancient learning.
I heard their urgent voices where I walked,

But took my love in my arms
And found a human music in her voice
And named as joy what they explored with law.

We are a new people, she and I,
Whose lilts are pagan and have no appointed sound.
Away and far down my ghosts whisper a weak song.

JANUARY POEM

Snow, Joan, has captured the garden
And frozen up its customary look.
A white witch's waste crawls from the window
Towards pure vertices of light,

While unsung silence menaces all thought -
The black masked window passes it inside;
Our piled communities are split to fiery bits
By the whitefall artist's slicing midnight grasp.

In this I write to tell you how the warmth
Of your whole being melts surrendered space,
Who are a glowing island in mysterious snow,
A source of sound in long regions of silence.

NORTH COUNTRY ARRIVAL

For three days after I arrived
The city lay happed in a thick fog,
So that it seemed I had come
To a strange country, where everything
Grew in spite of a choking disability.

On the fourth day it cleared,
And the buses moved and people went
About the streets with apparent purpose.
My thoughts were brought down to the level
Of sight, but I walked warily
Sensing the possibility of that grey return.

MOSAIC

Her craft is to fit stones
To make a bird, a prophet,
A huge face examined
By its cracks.

Of ways of making
This would seem most painful,
Stone by bit of coloured stone.

At distance the labour is concealed,
But draw near and something
Of the process talks up violently
In small squares that fight against
Their rhythms.

Which one of us could bear
Such naked art,
Who tick down and smooth
The flow of words
Lest our flaws cry out
In the terrible gaps of speech.

We stand in quarries
Where the stones come brittle
And the colours blear.

UNTITLED

Snapshots, mementoes of the glaring sun,
Paintings of yours that flame
The hard landscapes
                                        of Greece and Italy,
A southern brightness in the clutter
Of your winter room,
                                        that we are absent
From.
        Not, in your accurate recollections,
That waking in Paris,
                                        the long journey
Afterwards, south,
                                    and the wonder of you
That I am remembering.

POEM

She had a soft white skin,
Small breasts, merely, I thought,
'Like birds', and thighs
I did not seek images for.

Her walk when she came to me
Is indescribable.
I could not find words
For how she spoke.

Let this small, sudden nostalgia
Be her celebration.
These few lines, maybe without much passion,
Keep her on my page.

UNTITLED

In an east coast fishing village
I sat on a brown rock and watched
Four women lift their skirts
And wade into the sea.
Their legs gleamed white in the salt air,
Moving against the reiterated squeal of a gull,
And the clean retch of tide on the crisp sand.
In that slow silent procession
I saw across the empty beach
Four figures enter the legendary landscape
Of song bound kings, and ballad princesses.
Easily, easily in this land a little distance
Transforms the living and the dead into kingdoms
Of romance and wild splendour -
Even the blackest squalor of the foulest slums.

OLD THEME

Fathers all, I can meet you
Neither in old ghettos
Nor in newer suburbs
Of diaspora,

Nor even in restored Jerusalem;
But only across the Sambatyon,
That boiling, magic river,
Where the lost tribes live.

WOMAN FIGURE, SOUTH TURKEY

At hip height,
With wooden blocks held out for legs,
You occupy the pavement;
And as I meet your expression,
Arranged with silly sly hope among your fossiled limbs
I can't take what it expatiates about the
Human condition.

What shall I place between your lack and mine?

A shrewd determinist, the tourist knows the facts
Of economic conditions etc.,
And should be calm and objective,
(After all *I* don't live here)
Pass you a coin and remember you
Are part of the scenery.

What shall I place between your lack and mine?

In a spasm of fear I turn away
To cry down the men playing cards
Under the beautiful trees –
The harbour too is very beautiful –
And the draggle of filth
That overspreads my reason.

What shall I place between your lack and mine?

Down through those streets
A little way out on the blue water
There is a boat that goes a two days' journey
To my promised land.

I have no money left
To hold towards you.

What shall I place between your lack and mine?

In repeated visions some
Have seen even you comforted,
Taken into the arms of whatever
Monstrous god could mend
Your sores.
I can't get down to where love
Begins in you.
I can't
Easily pass you.

What shall I place between your lack and mine?

FOR CERTAIN IMMIGRANTS

The lives you have come up
Out of, I have not yet begun to understand.

I observe your thin boned elegant hands
Your love of colour, and hear
With a strange pleasure
The inimitable gutturals of your speech.

I see also your limbs shrivelled in weird poverties,

And I hear you stumble in a dialect of exile
That learned less, I think, than ours
How grief and pity could be diagnosed
And set down calmly in a classic style.

N.W.2 : SPRING

The poets never lied when they praised
Spring in England.
                                        Even in this neat suburb
You can feel there's something to
                                                                their pastorals.
Something gentle, broadly nostalgic, is stirring
On the well-aired pavements.
                                                        Indrawn brick
Sighs, and you notice the sudden sharpness
Of things growing.
                                        The sun lightens
The significance of what the houses
Are steeped in,
                                brightens out
Their winter brooding.
                                                Early May
Touches also the cold diasporas
That England hardly mentions.

ON A BALKAN VISA

In the south of that country I passed
Through a poverty I had never seen,
Where the people moved in postures
Of childishness, you could not even call
Despair.
            This was a peasanthood
That stood not hard against its land,
But slid and shuffled over it
With an empty look.
                        The importance
Of men who sat before boxes on which
They scrubbed their strength into other
People's shoes. The huddled bundles
In railway stations, that did not know
How to look or stand with human purpose.
The smell and decay of those below
Minimal significance.
                        Over this was
Cried Democracy, the People had been
Told of their own sovereignty.
                                Of compassion
No-one had told them, or explained
How they lay far below the beginning
Of such words.
                They had not even
The sharp hurts of children.

FOR J., IN HOLLAND

You are walking in a country I have never been to
So I do not know what you have become.

I move where we have been, remembering
Here you sat and smiled,
Here deeply thought and here
Frowned at my clumsy conversation.

I am afraid of what you will discover without me
As I am jealous of all love's unsound threats.

Will you come back to our familiar explorations,
Or return with glittering souvenirs
And the taste of foreign wines.

I ask only out of love
Which gives me over and over your image.
Return being that one gift, yourself.

NOTES FOR URIEL DA COSTA

b. Oporto c. 1590 – d. 1640, Amsterdam

Before adolescence I discovered you.
Now I can hardly recall the soulless terrors
Your tragedy gave
Me, the violence of your
Heresies,
            pitching through my childhood's
Talmud Torah.
                        Your fevers to believe,
Return and believe, grasped me
And pleaded for a pity I could never
Have defined.
                        Disgraced in the synagogue,
Excommunicated, I could shiver
At your drama,
                        your suicide seemed
An infinite passion.

                              But I have come now
Through books and books on laws and suffering,
And you are banished to a couple of pages
In Graetz's 'History'.
                              If I could, though,
I'd trace you out,
                        call up your anguish
That stalked the small scholar I was,
Recover what burned and moved me in your fate.

UNTITLED

One time as I was cycling along
The back road to Stow
I saw a small brown animal
Nuzzling at the bushes over the pulled up
Railway line.
                              At first I thought
It was a dog, but I could see from the way
It moved it was something different.
                                                            As I
Came closer I recognised it was a deer.

It went on eating softly for a little, but soon
Turned and jumped away down the bank

Into whatever mystery it had emerged from.

I never saw another.

UNTITLED

Having nowhere to be decently alone together
We carry our love through parks, through pubs
Through cheap Italian restaurants and secondhand bookshops.

UNTITLED

Out among the dormitory towns
Of Buckinghamshire we took a wrong turning
And lost our way.
                We stopped by a signpost
And discovered we were travelling
In a complete circle, without knowing how.
One of the girls made a joke about it
About us outside the ghetto, bewildered
In exile.
      Only a joke, of course.
                        The fields
Of the Home Counties at twilight don't
Look that hostile, and we're well provided
With maps.
        It was just a small diversion,
And we soon hit the right road again

But that moment we stopped was awkward, maybe
More than we said.

UNTITLED

Lately up in the Lake District
I took a walk from Keswick
To see the famous cataract
                                        of Lodore
Well, now the guidebook admits
The poet exaggerated.
                                        Where was
That stirring flow of water I've always

Wanted to witness since the words first
Cascaded through my classroom?
                                        I saw
Only a narrow strip of water, making
No great commotion.
                                        And all poets, I thought,
(As others have found) exaggerate, or worse,
And who does it matter to?

UNTITLED

Up there in Wordsworthshire, on a warm spring evening, I
    was drinking
In the shiny bar of a fairly posh hotel, two long, stringy

Haired hikers, with hippy faces, came in and made for the
    counter
But before they got there, the fairly smart Scotswoman
    behind it

Called out in a dry central lowland voice 'Ah'm sorry lads
But yull no' get served here.' They only looked a little

Thwarted, and went out. She waggled her bottom in a
Peculiar sort of respectably triumphant dance. She was

Reflecting, I suppose, the poet in his long later phase
Of settled gentility. But I, in keeping with most modern scholars

Am stirred by the decade or so of poems that plunge
Into obstinate questionings, especially of vagrants and the like.

DR ZAMENHOF

The inventor of Esperanto

I remember you also,
Who in Warsaw constructed words
You hoped we'd take, clean
Of the scratching, smeared connotations
We grow weird in
To speak with the heart of international man
The lonely accumulations
Of misheard humanity.

Ni ne parolas la Esperanton,
And you remain a high-thinking scholar
Who sketched a fragile, impossible dream
Over the impassioned wars of our condition
A kind of poor joke on our becultured selves.

You died, I think, before you could have seen
That makers of sound world language must provide
For the curious love of Yiddish and German
On the fields of Auschwitz.

PAINTER

We talked of Chagall tonight,
His curved red cow
That almost winks at you,
His lovers planted side by side
In the thick bouquets
Of the dancing villages
Of hard hasidic joy.

Walking home, I couldn't help it,
The moon sailed on a fiddle
In the sky. The traffic-lights
Danced green circles over the roofs.
From my feet the ground
Ran into poems the colour
Of this man's fervent world.

And my arms summoned
The climbing lilters of the streets
To a waved Sabbath, fresh as a new calf.

SABBATH MORNING: MEA SHEARIM

They came along the street, with huge fur hats,
Discussing, the soft bulks of prayer shawls
In their arms, or with the woollen maleness of shawls
Wrapped as holy armour round their backs,
And I was nearly seeing them as long ago, when
In the cold, wide synagogues I laid my shawl
And dreamed this way I would become a man.

SAMSON

Samson, that smashed the Philistines
And drove his anger through their stately homes,
Fell down in the soft appeal of those women
Whose skin was foreign to his consecrated fate.

The religion active in his blood
Suffered no frontiers their once mighty lords maintained.
He killed, ate and went to bed
To prove the gods don't always fawn on weakness,

And knew the man is cursed who is contained
And satisfied by his own people's mirrored greed:
Still was betrayed, blinded and enslaved
For a little evasion of his origin.

It was then no divine and marked up retribution
When he tore down the pleasureland of Gaza,
But the last act of a disencumbered man
Crazily striking the scene of his failure.

MENORAH

The symbol of this land is a seven branched
Candelabrum pressed up against the sun.

They ask me, the glowing ones, here,
'Does your heart hold up its fingers

Hard and alight, like our bare symbol?'
'My hand burns, here, my hand burns.'

TO A TEACHER OF HEBREW LITERATURE

You have no shame, you pronounce,
Like the shame of us who cling
To what, after all, we are:
Split at the foot of several cultures
And approved by none.

You are immensely satisfied to be where you are
And to have what you have.
No-one can touch you.

God, girl, your Israel is a ghetto
Narrower and more firmly surrounded
Than any we have known.
Its walls are built from an academic vision
Of a thing you have never felt.

Child, bone of my bone, flesh of my flesh,
When you speak of normality, of shame
Of cowardice, and of
The human ridge where we find being,
You play with things you do not understand.

OVER THERE, JUST HERE

From the observation post you can see them.
'It is quite safe', my friend says, 'only,
Do not point.
                    This barbed wire here
Is the frontier: that house just there belongs to them.
Sometimes you see a car jolt down that road.
It's an odd feeling.

Night-time their shadows light up with ours,
Go to bed with ours.
It's an odd feeling.

There has been no trouble now for four years.
Things have settled down to this unruffledness.
But don't point.'

BAB EL WAD

Limbs of trucks, hallowed
By a fierce sacredness,
Among the rocks of this gorge
Where in the small war
They were smashed
Lie in savage eloquence

In a dialect that disowns
Hillsides laid with trees,
Heavy with the spirit
Of European martyrdoms.

Bare iron driven on rock
Proclaims a posture of dying
That is of this land,
And it only.

Raw and sacred, death
Is proclaimed that we,
Inlaid with other death,
Are strange to.

BY KIRYAT SHEMONA

It was these hills in the beginning
Baked with fine purple and shaped
With sored cheeks of rock hacked out.
It was trails over these hills, the first
Forms.

Later is lost among codes
And poetry. What came down
To a significant wandering
In the desert, to an eventual
Sky of massacre is sunk
Beyond the cleverest probing.

But in the beginning,
Clearly and beyond speech, there were
These hills.

LESSON OF HISTORY

In my room at the crumbling edge
Of Jerusalem, I read far into the night
On the beginning of English history.

The invasions of Iberian, Celt,
Angle, Dane, Saxon, Norman and others
Forgotten, who swooped on the forests

And heath of that untracked island
Named it, and worked out a language
Suddenly shift out of lists I learned

At school. When the writer says 'horde'
I think I can see men descending from ships
Mounting the beaches and travelling inland.

When he says 'village', I think I feel
A collection of huts, men working the fields,
And a lord demanding and owning their labour.

Quaint dead customs, titles, loyalties
Spawn and settle out of chaos
I see the choices history confirms.

The sky, outside the cave of my room,
Is very clear. The stars can be told
By amateur astronomers.

Under the clear image of the sky, I wonder,
What forms breed here? What language grows?
Whose choice or action will endure

And shape the histories with schooled clichés?
If that comes will they be redeemed
More easily than in England - now?

ISRAELI ARAB

His English was smooth and graceful,
And his Hebrew better than mine
Will ever be. He talked charmingly
Of Nazareth his home town
And its centuries-old, strange customs.
But his gift for holding together
Politeness in several cultures concealed
An injury, and his voice turned
Attention to itself, by reaching
Towards tones we need never seek.
He was trying, of course, to make
The best of an impossible situation.
Meeting him that evening I was mostly silent,
Though I have access to three or four cultures, myself.

RELIGIOUS QUARTER

Grandfather, today I walked in Mea Shearim
And it was a little like it must have been
In Vilna seventy years ago.
                                        Small boys
Walked between their dangling curls
With already the strange sensuality of Talmud
Scholars. Merchants, in fur hats, relaxed
In the slow pace of their closed, coinless
Sabbath: matrons went with their love blown
Away into a nagging over-all welfare
And young girls were concealing their sex
In a terrible kind of shapelessness.
                                                    And all this
Under the hot sky of Jerusalem.

It was a little, grandfather, of the sea
Of the past, out of which you sailed
To leave me in the north,
                                        whose speech
I take to tame, oh, centuries of such
Isolated quarters striving in my blood.

LESSON NUMBER 24

This is a country where guns are known.
Not apparatus of pageantry,
But carried to use at the sudden edge
When suspicion lets its dogs leap free.

I shiver at them laid on a café table
Or one on a shoulder in the street.
Where I was born, in that careful island,
A gun was never a thing you could meet.

Here where the sky is clear and sharp
They're handled with exactitude.
Addressed with a sort of unprobed passion,
Can be the quick agents of a mood.

LOVE IN THIS BITTER SEASON

Love, in this bitter season
When life is disfigured
By an indecent mortality
Over your obvious silence
My love grows, close
To what grief has grown in you.

FOR THE *ANGLO-SAXON* POETS

To Robert Friend, Dennis Silk

The land needs skills.
Talents for construction, knowledge of machinery,
Methods for gathering statistical data,
All the expertness of the workshops
Of the most advanced sector of Exile
Are wanted, in their strictest application, here.

All the abilities are promised functions,
Are promised transformation, and the reward
Of endeavour in growing statehood.

But of our skill there is said nothing.
The immigration office has not found it necessary
To tempt out of the luxuries of the West
Its exiled poets, crying:
'Come we need your puzzlement.'

And we, after all, who have nevertheless
Brought such skill as we have for setting perception
In forms that generals don't give attention to,
And judges feel they can safely ignore,
Are accustomed to this sad lack of significance,

And you in your high Arab room on Abu Tor,
You in your tasteful basement in Jabotinsky,
And I in the wilderness of the Bokharan Quarter,

Surrounded by volumes of others who have
Got through a lifetime maintaining and shaping
These forms, can recall that they too have worked
In a deplorable absence of promotion.

How many states have felt they needed poets?

And yet these voices we have brought,
These voices that try to sing
As the best voices we heard in exile sang,
And still to be our own,
These words we break over the sardonic smile of the Negev,
Over the piety of Jerusalem,
Are our offering.

AFTERWARDS

Last night there were two jackals
Crying outside my door.
At first I did not recognise their pitiful sound,
Thinking it was human,
But by the way it hovered on the edge
Of the classes of pain
I placed it among the animal hills
Where I make no sense.

Afterwards, in the removal of their strange sound,
I could feel your cry,
That came against me without name
Or meaning I could place,
Except that your grief split this town
From end to end.
Tell me, did I tame it wrongly, now it has
Entered into words?

PORTRAIT

Yes, I can see most of it now.
It was an error to have read
In your face the things
That took me in.

Yes, this other in his painting
Has slashed you down
As nearly as the world
Sees you, as I should have seen.

And yet, however smoothly his paint
Sets this image of your face
My vision licks through it,
Changes its shaping tones, almost.

EARTHQUAKE

Our education
Was much taken up with theories of disaster,
'Atrocities'
Became a dulled word in our vocabularies.

Yet here the earth
Shivered and gaped to remind us of its own sort
Of offerings.

Old gods of the menace
In thunder and climbing floods, show us how to mourn
These ten thousand of your deaths.

PERHAPS . . .

Perhaps I can only mythologise what happened to you.
You had gone down into some stark underworld
To face an inconceivable terror. Then you stood
At the door with a wrist slashed, numbed with fear
Breaking a sensation of four heavy tablets.

The shuddering of this thing has gone. Now, there is
A calm square patch over the split mouth.
Your skin moves gently up into the light;
The stones of the street bruise if you touch them,
And if one looks clear into your eyes
Earth quivers there with startled innocence.

PATTERNS OF CULTURE

Behind the wire, unadorned with strangeness,
Was an ordinary pigeon,
The like of which has the freedom
Of Trafalgar Square.

Yet there among the poor rarities
Of the Belgrade Zoo
He was alien, therefore kept
On display out

Of the common air. 'But in London . . .'
I reacted. No-one stirred.
Between me and the dull grey pigeon
Were the habits of Yugoslavia.

HILLS

A wind grinding slow and fine
Over the black road. To my left
Clusters of light across the dark stones,
And on the right a high enclosure
Of military graves.
                    An eerie moment:
This is the country where miracles
Were in repute. An extraordinary
Flash met travellers on roads like this,
Blinding revelations disturbed the universe.

                    The moment passes.
I walk on in a restored darkness,
The road stretches where it has to.
Stones crunch firm-edged under my feet.

The stars stay shining apart, though,
Distant, given to mystery.

CLASSIC

Odi et Amo: I know
Just how Catullus felt,
And am no more able
To explain it.

I can't bear you
And want you with me
Against perpetual night.

CRISIS

(*To Z.G.*)

You, I suppose, wouldn't remember this.
We were outside Tsfat
on a clear, blue
Summer day.
A huge bird entered
The sky above our
hillside. It was empty
Except for this dark
bird that had
The whole sky
to fly in. It swooped
And poised
over where we were
Then moved
away to some other
Abstract point
in the sky. There was
No wind
to carry it, only
The innate
power of its black wings.
It had
its own motives, in that
Blue, blue
sky. It hovered over us
On the curl
of its black wing.

SO ALWAYS

So always a dark past surrounds me
With its figures broken across strange tongues
And places unreconciled. I am moved
By what I cannot fathom, hurt by what
I cannot hold.
                    Yet it is no mere theme
Of unresolved longing I follow in the shifting
Trappings of my verse.
                              It is no lost look
At a fabulous kingdom I hunt down.

                              What I hold after is an
Image of the sad, piercing lyric, the mighty
Beaten faith that fires my blood,

                              That was never yet gathered,
Trim and labelled, in the courts of style.

HERE

My face is white, but
It so easily might not have been.
My tongue is English, but
It so easily might not have been.
This town is peaceful, but
It so easily might not have been.
My poems are as they are, because
It so easily might not have been.

AFTERNOON BY A KIBBUTZ

Where the hills end there is a rich farmland,
Yellow corn sways in curving mass against
Deep green grass, and the ploughed up land draws
Its brown ridges towards the shade of a patch
Of trees planted in a thin cool line at
The side of the glittering road. The railway
Tracks gleam in the sunlight. Olive trees writhe
Their grey muscled trunks in eloquent forms.
A dead stream straggles under a white bridge.
An Arab ruin crumbles on a hill. A
Cement factory puffs up its soft smoke into
The unmoved blue. Further, halfway up a slope
Are the green, frail huts of a settlement
Where some are trying to establish absolute
Equality, necessary kinds of links.

TONGUE

It can come lowpin' up in me an' a',
This wey o' talkin'.
I dinnae ken whit tae dae wi' it
But it's there richt eneuch.

UNTITLED

Back in Manchester, after a long time,
I saw the streets where the Jews used to live
Are derelict, disappearing.

That unwalled ghetto is being
Transported, dispersed
Into some kind of elegance.

And Whitechapel, too, is being made over
New roads and tall blocks
Cut across old clusterings
Of aspiration.

The Gorbals, it's said, is rising
In skyscrapers.

Why should I not celebrate
Such rehousing,
Such furthering of diaspora?

THE SKUAS

(*For Pirjo*)

It hardly seemed believable
that those birds
Would come for us,
but they did, swooping
Into our faces,
then up, turning and steadying
On black and white wings,
aiming, and down again
There was a war between us
and the taut
intelligences
We stood still and fascinated,
intruders, exposed

UNTITLED

Among these green hills
And weaving lanes
Clear sunsets
Bring back Jerusalem
And I don't know
Whether it is earthly Jerusalem
Under whose walls
I lived for three years long ago
Or some earlier Jerusalem
Whose vision moved me
In this country
Longer ago.

UNTITLED

It's as though someone took an axe
To my writing desk

My work's chopped up, scattered

Much lost.

After this savaging, what is there
To find among the damage?

WHAT ARE YOU TALKING ABOUT?

Afterwards, as we know,
There are those who virtuously
Declare: We didn't know.

Things happened somewhere else,
Or didn't happen like that,
Or we weren't really told.

Anyway, we had no power
To alter or divert
What did or didn't go on.

It's a familiar sound
To be heard among us now,
The deceiving whine of those
Who participate and know.

HITCHING

We used to curse all the cars
That calmly passed us by
As we waited often
In unrelenting weather.

But those that didn't stop
Were right,
After all.

We weren't going anywhere,
Together,
You and I.

PLACE

Let me speak about diaspora,
The long exile burning in us,
Burning out.
                    It is the thing,
Maybe, that draws and lets us
Talk to one another intimately
In the dark,
                  but in the light
We don't always say what we have to:
Our words are not ours.
                                 Hold me,
Love, in the light as in darkness,
As I hold you, in exile,
Home with you, wherever we are.

DEAR MR LEONARD

I wonder whether you'd be
Interested,
But one Saturday afternoon
During the course of a religious discussion
An aunt of mine remarked to me:
'Ah'm no froom
Bit whan Ah see them
Ee'in the trayfi meat
It scunners me.'
I found this very striking
And it occurs to me
You could use it
In one of your poems.
Anyway, you might want to
Think about it.

IN EDINBURGH AGAIN

There was a clear pink in the sky over Arthur's Seat
But Princes Street seemed swollen with mist.
You couldn't see Fife. Frost bit the pavements
And the city touched its cold morning.

I walked round, waiting to phone you,
To bring back the stark, grey buildings,
The place of our love.

ISOLATION

While we've hardly noticed it the leaves have turned
Yellow, golden, brown and richly red.
The trees hum delicately with autumn
And seem to ask the tawny question,
Shall we last out here the winter?

EDINBURGH NEW TOWN

In Heriot Row, on a misty November evening
When the lamps were lit early in the cold damp,
We passed the house of Stevenson, and found
A metal plaque outside with a stanza of the poem
About Leerie we both knew.
                                        We were glad
To remember that 'Child's Garden of Verses'
It came from, glad to remember the way
It was read to us, or we read it, long ago.

A most Stevensonian evening (was it not?)
As we walked along the pavement of that fine terrace,

Back through our childhoods, in those suburbs
That brought us together, and drove us apart.

HÖLDERLIN

This autumn morning cannot glow so bright
As memory of it
Will flare on a winter's day
Then shall I find anguish
Gazing from your tower on the livid water

REPORT

Suddenly, I read in a newspaper
About an Arab poet,
Whose name I've never heard of,
Whose work I don't know,
In the land of Israel, in Palestine,
Fined, suppressed, threatened with imprisonment
For 'incitement',
And I want to shout:
Let his poetry survive in its valley
Making nothing happen,
Let him demonstrate his types of ambiguity,
Let him speak awkwardly, inadequately,
Like the rest of us,
For himself.

UNTITLED

My typewriter is old and dusty,
But everything about it fascinates

    You like the asterisk best
(I told you it was a star)
And are gratefully thrilled
With everything I let you press.
'What does this do?' you ask
'And that?' What a machine –
It is where so many things move.

UNTITLED

From Oban the islands drift away
Into the Gaelic West
                        They're out there now
Beyond the bay,
                with all their dying
Culture
        rubbed out
                    almost past
The point of revival.
                        There's not much left
To sail in, across the blue waters
Of the Hebrides.

TRIOLET

Are there poets from the floor?
John Rety asks at Torriano
Just read one piece, please, no more.
Are there poets from the floor,
New or having read before?
Go up and stand beside the piano
Are there poets from the floor,
John Rety asks at Torriano?

ROMANCE

In the film
(As far as I remember)
The Italian soldier
Was impressing on his Spanish prisoner
In the civil war
The right pronunciation of the name of the cigarettes
The latter had cadged.

Matchedonia,
He intoned
But it slithered out
Mathedonia from the Spaniard, naturally.

I appreciated both pronunciations,
But because of you
The sneeze of Tuscany
Was much less familiar
Than the lisp of Castile.

IN MADRID

I still remember
Sitting on the balcony of your old flat
And watching the swallows flying
Around the factory opposite.

I don't know

Whether they stopped to look at us
Or learned our names

(Like those in Bécquer's poem).

For me, anyway,
They're ones which return.

ABOUT MAKING

It is as well to be careful,
To pare down statement,
To keep close
To the unsayable.

But also to bear in mind
There is deliberate silencing,
To speak up against it
To make oneself heard.

1492

Descubrimiento o encuentro,
Discovery or encounter,
La leyenda negra o la leyenda rosa,
The black legend or the rosy one,
Which shall I go for?

Look, I am no historian
Or acknowledged scholar.

I can't choose easily between such terms,
Yet feel their resonance.

I am compelled to think of fields
Where terms evaporate
And concentration ends.

UNTITLED

Despite the real spite
And making nothing happen
What is it that survives?

Rhythm imperfectly recognised
A feeling for words
Craftily organised,
Emotion collected with fragility.

And what is the reaction?
Too little recognition or too much
Of a wrong kind.

Despite the real spite,
Continue.

Something may penetrate,
Something inaudible otherwise
May be heard.

CUTTING DOWN

A whole forest of beech trees toppled.
They look so naked and helpless
Those smooth, grey trees that the saw
Lowers in an instant.
                                        Perhaps it's absurd
To pity trees, perhaps the 'timber operations'
(As a sign puts it) are necessary.
                                                        But
When we first came to the valley
The wood was there at the roadside,
A graceful landmark we took for granted.
                                                                    Now, suddenly,
There's only an empty slope,
                                                    whose surroundings
Seem shamefaced, awkwardly open.

READINGS

er sind
noch lieder zu singen jenseits
der Menschen
(Paul Celan)

there are
still songs to be sung on the other side
of mankind
(tr. by Michael Hamburger)

I try to believe it:
I see myself put my hand
Through the wire, groping
Among mashed alphabets.

Is this piece I've dragged out an A?
Does this look something like a D?
Could this be another A?
Would you say this was an M?

LOVE POEM

Blessed are you, my dearest, queen of my universe,
Who touch all things with light.

UNTITLED

All poets are Jews,
Tsvetaeva said.

When the fury and spite
Of the loudly virtuous
Build up around me
(Oh it happens, I assure you)
I can't always tell
Whether it's the Jew in me
Or the poet
They've got their sights on.

Hatred, anyway, is hatred
And always comes
To the same thing.

ETHICS

No, I can't say what it is,
The right measure
Between individual and community.

I acknowledge an inability
To legislate.

I'd also like to quote Hillel,
Who asked:

'If I am not for myself,
Who is for me?

And being for myself,
What am I?

And if not now, when?'

TRANSLATIONS
FROM THE HEBREW
PUBLISHED IN BOOK FORM

David Vogel, The Dark Gate, 1976
Avraham Ben-Yitzhak, Eleven Poems, 1994

Note:

David Vogel never used titles for individual poems.
In this book the poems are numbered.

David Vogel

I

Days were great as lakes
And clear
For we were children.

We sat a long time on their banks
And played,
Or went down to swim
In the fresh water.

And sometimes we wept
In our mother's apron,
For life was filling us
Like jugs of wine.

II

You sit here beside me
And our shadows grow bigger than we are.

The candle is going out.
Happiness has come and gone.

Our hearts hurt us,
We sit sadly
Like children punished by the rabbi.

You sit here beside me,
And our shadows grow bigger than we are.

III

Our childhood spilled into our hearts
A deep, sweet grief –
How distant it is now!

The Talmud chant,
Heavy with dreams and longing,
Still rises at times,
Unsought, to our lips.

We look back
Anguished
At our startled innocent hearts
Almost in recognition.

We wander through life
Weeping,
With empty palms
Held out, shaking,
To every passer-by.

IV

A silent evening will flow
Through the window
And fill the room.

Under a heap of strange shadows,
Beside a black silence
I shall lie
And my heart will ache
And ache.

From the distance
A lonely trumpet plays bright songs
Of childhood.

And my far-off, forgotten
Village
Will draw near my bed softly
To stretch out at my feet.

Under a heap of strange shadows,
Beside a black silence
I shall lie
And my heart will ache
And ache.

V

An autumn day will breathe.
With a pale, trembling hand
It will slowly strip the black dress
From your sleeping village.

In front of your white house
The naked linden tree will stand
Sadly swaying.

I shall come back lonely
Out of the night
Bow gently to her and say:
'Take my greeting to your mistress'

But you
Will go on softly sleeping on your couch.

VI

How can I see you, love,
Standing alone
Amid storms of grief
Without feeling my heart shake?

A deep night,
Blacker than the blackness of your eyes,
Has fallen silently
On the world,

And is touching your curls.

Come,
My hand will clasp your dreaming
Hand,
And I shall lead you between the nights,

Through the pale mists of childhood,
Thus my father guided me
To the house of prayer.

VII

On summer evenings
Blue mists
Sometimes rise
From streams
And hang trembling
Among evening whisperings.

Sometimes the wind dips into them,
And lightly touches our nostrils
With flavours of sharp perfumes.

At the edges of forests
Young girls sit by themselves
With their hair hanging loose
Weeping sweet tears
Over nothing.

Let me go then,
Silent, in the footsteps of the summer evenings
In my hidden soul
The evenings tremble
Invisibly quivering
Over nothing.

VIII

With gentle fingers
The rain is softly
Playing sad melodies
On the black instrument of night.

Now we are sitting in the darkness,
Each in his own house
(The children have fallen asleep)
Listening quietly to the rain
Telling our sorrow.

For we have no more words.
Our feet have been leadened
By day.
There is no dance
Left in them.

IX

I saw my father drowning
In surging days.
His weak hand gave a last white flutter
To the distance –
And he is gone.

I kept on alone
Along the shore,
A boy still,
With small, thin legs,
And have grown as far as this.

And now I am my father,
And all those waves
Have broken over me,
And left my soul numb.

But all I held holy
Have gone into the wilderness
And I stretch out a hand to no one.

I am happy to rest
In the black cradle of night,
Over me the sky's canopy,
Studded with silver.

X

Black flags are fluttering
In the wind
Like the wings of caged birds.
All of us, for many days and nights,
Will go secretly,
Downcast,
Till we come
To the great, dark gate.

Like ignorant children
We shall stand there nervously
Waiting
For the opening
Of the great, dark gate.

XI

The ship is far away from us.
The waters will darken into night,
But we must row and row.

Two old men said in their hearts
On a summer's day at its height:
The grandchildren romp
Like young lions in play.
For us it is good to rest
From our load of years.

When the sky turns blue for morning
Let the children go on sleeping
Till the black ship has passed.

XII

Through black night
The journey will sweep
Taking me somewhere.

The carriage will fill slowly
With heavy snoring.

A faint, solitary light will glow
For an instant, far away,
And vanish.

Where, love, will you be then?

A dark river will be whispering,
Perhaps, as I go.

A dead station will throw
A look of longing after me.

Through black night
The journey will sweep.

XIII

Children are playing beside the fence.
Summer noon is striding, heavy and silent,
Through the village.

Suddenly a cock's curving cry
Shatters the silence
Like a golden arc of lightning
In the sky's blue depth.

The fathers are out of sight.
Each is at his work.

A shaggy, black dog
Sprawls in the shadow of the fence.
Its tongue hanging out limply,
It makes a pink movement in the shadow.

The children play on, lazily,
A fly goes zooming,
Zooming round.

XIV

These great, silent houses
I must bear alone
Now all my brothers have left.

In the darkness of side-streets
Days will crumble, sunless.
No one will weep for them.

Yesterday we were children.
Our mothers used to wipe the sweat of play
From our faces.

Where are you all hiding,
My swift colts?

Autumn is hurrying on.
I can hear his steps through the leaves on the avenue.
By morning he will be at my house.

XV

Plain, humble letters
A heavy hand laboured to write
I have draped like decorations on my chest.

Your words sprouted in Bessarabian plains
Like tough stalks of maize,
My dark sister.

In front of your door you dug a well:
Your neighbour's shaggy dog
Came to watch,
And in the evening
Your children tried to catch in it
A coaxing moon.

When I was a crawling baby
You kept me from falling
Off the table.

And now I speak strange words
Every night
To the surprised city.
And no one knows
I am talking inwardly to you,
My sister, hidden
In Bessarabian plains.

XVI

Through countless generations
You've come to stay with me.
You are very young
And sleep all day.

From your half-lit past a world will grow for you,
With bears and lambs and fabulous creatures,
And laughter will light up your slumber.

Already in your flesh you are conceiving me,
And when you wake, my blessing,
I shall go with you to the farthest shores of life,
I and my father and the first man.

XVII

Don't be frightened, my son
They are only two mice
Jumping off the table to the chair.
They're smaller than you
And can't eat you.

Don't be frightened, my son,
It's only the rain's finger
Tapping, damp, on the window,
We won't let him in.

Hide snug in me,
I am your mother.
The dark night will stretch over us,
And no one will find us.

XVIII

Sometimes from far away
Pleasant, brown-backed autumns
Pass in front of me again
And their forgotten scent rises in my nostrils
Through cracks in a white winter

We used to walk slowly alongside the horizon,
By evening skies
That glowed green
And became red,
Like the cheeks of an apple.

The scent of a ripe world was silently carried,
From newly threshed corn,
From heavy fruit.
Tired pears
Dropped invisibly to the ground.

Cattle came back
Well warmed from the summer;
Women were swelling
With new children.

We felt a sadness
As the brown evening spilled over us
And the wind softly stroked our hair.

But a joy was hidden
Within us
And it still beats ashamed in our hearts
When we see the path
Of those distant autumns again
Through cracks in a white winter.

XIX

When I was growing up, troubled and reckless,
My father told me, God, about you.

But I ran away from you
To play,
For there was so little time.

And you
Always wisely kept hidden
So as not to spoil my games,
Till I'd almost forgotten you.

And now as I come back home alone
(All my companions fell asleep along the road)
I've made you out walking beside me,
Old and poor,
As I am today.

I'll lend you my stick
As far as a bench in the evening park.
We'll gently inhale the purple smell
Of far-off skies,
And watch the children playing further
And further away form us.

Then we shall turn to the evening,
We together and on our own,
To rest.

XX

Now I have forgotten all
The cities of my youth,
And you in one of them.

Through puddles of rainwater
You still dance for me, barefoot,
Though you must be dead.

How I rushed galloping
Out of my distant childhood
To reach the white palace of age
That is huge and empty.

I can't see back
To the start of my journey,
Or back to you,
Or myself as I was.

The path of days
From a distance
Continues to move
From nowhere to nowhere,
Without me.

XXI

I shall come back to your quiet fields,
Sheltered by evening,
With nothing in my hands.

My world perished in the world's strife.
All those near to me turned away,
For I became very poor.

And now I come in my poverty
Kneeling to you,
Ashamed and humbled,
That your forest may pour its stillness
Into my empty spirit,
As it did before.

Avraham Ben-Yitzhak

NIGHTS TURNED WHITE

In those white dream nights
The tired world dreams,
Quietened time may attend to its own pulse beat
Among springs' loud music,
Made of the song of their self.

Past and future turn completed,
For the present is a lasting calm.
In your life's silence
Stars grow quiet.
A wind sweeps from the everlasting:
Your eyes widen.

AUTUMN IN THE AVENUE

Lights that are dreaming,
Lights whitening,
At my feet are falling;
Shadows that are soft,
Tired shadows,
Fondle my path.

Between bared tree heights
A little wind
Moves sound
And hushes.
A last leaf
Floats downwards,
Trembles for one moment –
Then turns to silence.

WHILE DAY SINKS

Let us take off from our foreheads, as the red
Fires of our lives die down, the festival garlands
With their wild leaves and falling roses,
And silently go down to the rivers.

While daylight sinks, let us stand
On their banks, watching as they flow
Proud and neglected in their endless isolation.

In the red wash of dusk,
Surprised, we shall see there are flowers,
White flowers
Carried gently on the face of the water
From the corner of the garden
Where they were carelessly flung
At noon.

We shall realise we saw our youth passing.
While the memory sets in our souls
The sad shadow of the willows will darken on our heads.

Yet over us star after star will march on the hills,
A great strange night come down
And an evening wind touch us with the sound of black harps.

THERE IS A NIGHT THE STORM

There is a night the storm crosses your black land,
Slashing the power of soaking leaved forests,
Warms fields' breathing,
Strips rivers bare, flaying their nakedness,
And drawing mist.

In such a night
It forces with a wheezing gasp towards your walls,
Shifts suddenly back to the forest,
And then comes back in a thin whistle
To shatter your door and burst through your attic.
Its laughter's wailing lifts you from the burning arms of dreams.
Its cold flight touches your hot forehead
And it moves on howling.
You lie
With your body heavy and lost, with a parched soul,
And you strain listening
Wide-eyed, imprisoned in night.

Till a young day comes, its face pale,
Its eyes gazing at the world in wonder.
Your sad yearnings grope towards it,
But you tremble
For lack of understanding –
Tonight spring went over you
In the passing of the storm.

PSALM

There are a very few moments when you
Lift your soul within you like a drop of crystal.
The world is filled with its sun and broken colours,
Collection of sights and trembling objects,
And you perceive the world
As the drop of crystal.
Yet your world strains quivering to pour out,
Not to remain full,
Towards all limits, quivers.
You are given to all worlds.
The ends of stretches of air flow from your eyes,
Fears of darkness crouch in them,
Distant and close things find you
And demand your soul.

Stand, in night's silence,
On mountain summits,
Among the big cold stars lay your head.
The lives below you sink to the ground,
On the last burning of their grief
A black oblivion comes down.
You, though, wake to terrors
Above the darkness.
If a star drops
Through fear of the flamed roar
Rising from the distress of oblivion to the sky
It falls in the depths of your soul
And is consumed.

In the coming of morning
You are hovering over the face of the deep,
Drawing over it your profound heaven,
With the great sun in your hands
Till evening.

I DIDN'T KNOW MY SOUL

In this vintage season, when the skies are full of movement,
Rays of light are thrown out by the earth,
Gray, wasting clouds are driven
Wide winged by the storm.
From the greenish black of the forest
Your house emerges doubly pale in its isolation,
Calling me with its windows:
In my heart
Is shelter from the storm.

When you are sitting by the hearth,
And its gold dances
On the deep brown of your bent head,
Light flows between your fingers,
And the flame reflects movement
In the black silk of your dress.
Silently apples lie burning on your table,
Yellow grapes cluster thickly in their basket,
There is the full scent of blessing.

Let the forest thunder and roar,
Its song is sweet
In the stillness
Of your loved corner.
You and I,
With the sea's din
Over us,
Concealed
Like two pearls
Embroidered
On the bed of the sea.

I didn't know my soul.
It took its fill of silence.
Look, my spirit's wings flutter.
The forest may roar and thunder,
The wind strike its waves,
While your quivering look rests on me.
In you is blessing
And comfort,
Though the storm cried at my soul,
Listen, there is a howling of breakers in the forest,
The whole earth is cried on;
The world has set all its soul bare
Before God in the storm.

BRIGHT WINTER

The world is pure, hard and white.
The wind from the north yesterday scattered
The purposeless,
Blind and wandering
Dreams of mist.
Today the wind holds back its breath.
All round snow glints,
Deep blue shadows are on the mountains,
The pale blue skies
In their light, quiver.
In shadow,
The river extends
Trapped in its frozen beauty,
Ice of dimmed emerald
And bright glowing snows,
Till its curved green
Track is lost, there
In distance.
Daylight takes fire there
And its pieces of flame glitter
As though a sun had fallen
On mass ice figures,
Hardened like crystal,
And been broken.
I close my eyes.
My blood in me
Makes music, rings
In my ears:
The world is pure.

It feels
As though my own heart
Beats with the earth's heart,
And travels the streams
That flow under the pelt of ice.

A pure world,
Pure.

BLESSED ARE THOSE WHO SOW AND DO NOT REAP

Blessed are those who sow and do not reap
Because they wander far.

Blessed are those who give themselves freely, the splendour
Of whose youth has added to daylight
Though they flung off their glory where roads part.

Blessed are those whose pride crosses the borders of their souls
And becomes a white humility
After the rainbow's rising in the cloud.

Blessed are those who know what their heart cries out in deserts
And on whose lips silence flowers.

Blessed are they, for they will be taken into the heart of the world
Wrapped in a cloak of unremembrance,
Forever remaining without speech.

KINGDOM

The daylight flickers on my crown,
Whose gold burdens my forehead,
The edges of my robe wash over the marble staircase,
The sea moans its fine evening grief.

Night's daughter, come quietly,
Sit at my feet on marble whiteness.
Let the wind lift your hair,
Such black hair.
The waters are rising:
Stay quiet
Till I tell you: Get up and sing.

THE MOUNTAINS GROUPED AROUND MY TOWN

The mountains standing grouped around my town
Have a secret hidden in their forests:
There is the sea of trees' rushing above
And in shadow, below, the hidden secret.
Came vintage
With gold force
And scattered light around.
All the narrow tracks lightened.
The forest took on brightness.
It was tall and quiet,
Head in the sky.
Over its secret
Rests light.

THE LONELY SAY

One day leaves a flickering sun for the next,
Night mourns night.
Summer after summer is gathered in falling leaves
While the world sings its pain.

Tomorrow we shall die and have no more speaking
As the day we set out, face a gate closing.
When the heart exults it is God who draws us,
But fearing sacrilege – repents.

One day lifts a burning sun for the next,
Nights pour out their stars.
A few lonely lips hold their song.
On seven paths we are divided, return by one.

A PREFACE TO THE POEMS OF AVRAHAM BEN- YITZHAK

A. C. Jacobs

The translations reprinted here were done at the beginning of the sixties in Jerusalem. I had gone to Israel, intending to spend a few weeks there, but my stay lengthened into three years. As well as writing my own poems, it seemed natural to use the knowledge of Hebrew I had in attempts at rendering modern poetry into English.

It seemed a time when things were opening up in translation from Hebrew. Influential figures like Avraham Shlonsky, Nathan Alterman and Leah Goldberg (poets of the second generation who began the process of domesticating Hebrew poetry after the founding fathers, Bialik and Tchernikhovsky, had revived it) were still very much around. Brooding over all was the massive figure of Uri Zvi Greenberg, whose angry epic flow compelled respect even among those who disliked the sound of his unmixed wrath.

There was also a younger generation of poets establishing itself, beginning with Amir Gilboa, and including names such as Yehuda Amichai, Natan Zach and Dan Pagis, who began to use Hebrew as a spoken language in ways that had not been possible before. It felt as though there was a lot of work lying in wait for translators, and there was official encouragement, pressure even, for it to be done. One could think of oneself as a *chalutz* in translation, the equivalent of those pioneers who 'went up', as it was put, to renew and cultivate the land.

The Israel of those years was geographically different from today. There were no territories and Jerusalem was a divided city. The Old City was, and remains, unknown to me. Before 1967, western, Jewish Jerusalem was a small quiet town, which still kept some of its British colonial feeling, very different from the rush of Tel Aviv.

The world, however, or at least its reporters and

broadcasters, came to Jerusalem while I was there, for the trial of Adolf Eichmann, whose activities had affected so many people around.

I do not remember how I first became aware of Avraham Ben-Yitzhak's poetry, whether I knew of him before I went to Jerusalem or discovered his work there. In any case, no one interested in recent Hebrew poetry could have failed to hear of him in Israel at that time.

He was spoken of as a master craftsman, someone who knew how to shape Hebrew verse with unusual delicacy, who avoided the rhetorical drive that seemed to swell out of so much modern Hebrew poetry. To some he was the object of something like a cult of purity as though he had written poetry perfectly untouched by mundane and vulgar things, but this attitude rather repelled me and seemed wrong.

Others said that unlike most poets of the Hebrew revival, Ben-Yitzhak's slim volume had followed German poetic tradition rather than Russian, and his work could be related to the Expressionist modernist movements in central European poetry. Others still, liked his work because although written in Hebrew, it did not, for them, seem Jewish, a matter which has haunted some Israeli readers and writers.

However his work may have been seen then, the man himself was still remembered personally. He had died ten years earlier. People often spoke in particular of Leah Goldberg's love for him, a love that was more obvious and well known.

I bought a copy of Avraham Ben-Yitzhak's necessarily slim *Collected Poems* in one of Jerusalem's many bookshops. . .

[The unfinished manuscript was found in Madrid. In Angela Fuertes' words: "Arthur was writing this preface to the volume of his forthcoming translations of Avraham Ben-Yitzhak's poems when he collapsed.". JR.]

TRANSLATIONS
UNCOLLECTED IN BOOK FORM
&
UNPUBLISHED TRANSLATIONS

Hayyim Nahman Bialik

WHEN THE DAYS GROW LONG

When the days grow long, each one an eternity,
Each one as alike as yesterday and the day before it,
Just days, without much pleasure and filled with dullness,
And men and animals are seized by boredom,
A man will go out at sunset to walk on the seashore,
And see that the sea has not fled,
And he will yawn,
And go to the Jordan, and it will not flow back,
And he will yawn,
And see the Pleiades and Orion, not budging from their
    places,
And he will yawn;
And men and animals will sit, bored, together,
With their lives weighing heavily upon them,
And men will pluck the hairs of their head in distraction,
And cats will lose their whiskers.

Then the longings will rise,
Rise of themselves – like mushrooms raising a stench
In a decaying plank of wood.
The longings will fill all cracks and crevices,
As lice fill rags.
And when a man comes back to his hut for his supper,
And dips his crust and his salt herring in vinegar,
He will long,
He will drink his cup of murky, lukewarm water
And he will long;
He will take off his shoes and socks by his bed,
And he will long;
Man and animal both will sit in longing:
The man will wail in his dreams from his vast longing,

While the cat, on the tin roof, yells and scratches.
Then the hunger will come,
Growing, increasing, like nothing before it,
Not hunger for bread or vision, but for the Messiah.

And early in the morning, with the sun not quite showing,
The man, exhausted, shaken, glutted with dreams and
empty in spirit,
The webs of an angry sleep still on his eyelids,
The night's dread in his bones,
Will get up from his bed, from the darkness of his hut,
And with the cat still wailing, its nails
Still grating on his brain and on his nerves,
He will hurry to his window and wipe off the steam,
Or he will get up and go to the entrance of his shack
And, shading his eyes with his hand, look out, blearily,
fevered
And hungry for salvation, towards the little path behind
his yard,
Towards the slope of the rubbish heap opposite his home,
Looking for the Messiah;
And under the blanket, the woman will wake, uncovering
herself,
Her hair all wild, her body chafed, and her spirit murky,
And, pulling her shrivelled nipple from her baby's mouth,
She will turn and listen very carefully:
Isn't the Messiah coming?
Hasn't anyone heard his donkey braying?
And the infant will look out of its cot,
And the mouse will peep out of its hole:
Isn't the Messiah coming?
Has no one heard his donkey's jingling bell?
And the maid, heating the kettle on the stove,
Will stick out her sooty face:
Isn't the Messiah coming?
Has no one heard the sound of his horn?

AFTER MY DEATH

After I am dead
Say this at my funeral:

There was a man who exists no more.

That man died before his time
And his life's song was broken off halfway.
Oh! But he had one more poem
And that poem has been lost,
Lost for ever.
Oh! But he had a lyre,
And a vital, quivering soul.
Whenever he spoke with the lyre
He gave it all his heart's secrets,
His hand struck all its chords.
But there was one secret he kept hidden
Though his fingers danced everywhere.
One string stayed mute
And is still soundless.
Oh! But all its days
That string trembled,
Trembled softly, softly quivered
For the poem that would free her,
Yearned and thirsted, grieved and wept,
As though pining for someone expected
But he does not come,
She waits for him every day,
And the more he delays,
The more she whimpers
With a soft, fine sound,
And he delays,
But does not come,

And the agony is very great,
There was a man and he exists no more.
His life's song was broken off halfway.
He had one more poem
And that poem is lost,
For ever.

ON YOUR DESOLATE HEARTS

In the destruction of your hearts, the *mezuzah* is defiled,
And demons dance and hold their revels there.
That crew of mockers, worthless and reviled,
Raise shouts of joy and tempests in the air.

But, do you see, there's someone by the door,
Holding a broom. He is, you know, *shamash*
Of wrecked temples - Despair, who drives the furore
Of all that crew away with, 'Out, you trash!'

The flame flickers out in the last of your fires.
Your sanctuary's dumb, its mob all gone,.
But on your hearts' altar's desolate burnt pyres
A horrific cat goes yawning, howling, on and on.

ON THE TOP OF A HOLY MOUNTAIN

On the top of a holy mountain, his arms raised high,
An old man has been standing in silence, since the world was
young.
In his left hand he holds a great rod, and in his right huge stones;
His face shines in glory, at his waist tall clouds are hung,

While at his feet two massive giants lie beaten down,
oppressed.
Struggling fiercely with him they battle again and again:
With axes and spears they go on trying to climb to his height
And steal his stone tablets, but they try in vain.

His eyes shine out like the first bright light of dawn,
As he looks down at them his gaze is pure and meek,
While the giants are crushed and beaten to their knees –
Be mute in his great presence. He is singular, unique.

Yehuda Amichai

ON THE DAY OF ATONEMENT JERUSALEM 1967

On the Day of Atonement 1967 I put on
My dark festival clothes and went to the Old City of
    Jerusalem.
I stood a long time in front of the lowly shop of an Arab,
Not far from the Shechem Gate, a shop that had
Buttons and clasps and cotton-reels
Of all colours, and zips and buckles.
A rare light and many colours, like an Ark of the Law, opened.

In my heart I told him that my father
Also had a shop like that with buttons and cotton.
In my heart I explained to him all the decades
And causes and events, that set me here now,
While my father's shop lies burnt there, and he is buried here.

As I was finishing it was time for the Closing Prayer.
And he too pulled down his shutters and closed his door
And I with all the other worshippers went home.

THE TOWN I WAS BORN IN

The town I was born in was wiped out by guns,
The ship I immigrated on was later sunk in the war,
The barn in Hamadiya where I made love burned down.
The kiosk at Ein Gedi was blown up by the enemy,
The bridge at Ismailia I used to cross
Back and forth on the eve of my loves
Got smashed to pieces.

My life's erased behind me like a precise map.
How long will my memories hold on?
They killed the girl who shared my childhood,
And my father's dead.

So don't pick me for a lover or son,
A crosser of bridges, a tenant or a citizen.

THE FIRST BATTLES

The first battles grew
Fearful love flowers
With almost lethal kisses, like shells.
In the fine buses of our city
The soldier lads are driven away:
All routes, 5, 8, 12,
Finish at the front.

RAIN ON THE BATTLEFIELD

Rain falls on the faces of my friends;
On the faces of living friends, who
Cover their heads with blankets,
And on the faces of dead friends, who
Don't cover themselves up any more.

SYNAGOGUE IN FLORENCE

Spring softness in the synagogue yard,
A tree in blossom and four little girls playing
In between their lessons in the holy tongue
In front of a memorial wall made of marble:
Levi, Sonnino, Cassuto and others
In straight lines as in a newspaper
Or Torah scroll.

And the tree isn't there in remembrance of anything
Except remembrance of this spring,
Arrivederci, Our Father,
Buona notte, Our King.

There are tears in the eyes
Like dry crumbs in the pocket
From a cake that once was.

Buona notte, Sonnino,
Arrivederci, six million,
And little girls, and trees and crumbs.

A. L. Strauss

LAMENT FOR THE EUROPEAN EXILE

The thin mask of my sleep
Caught fire.
I woke
With my face seared.
I had seen the flames of the sunset,
But this was a new sun,
A red sun
That lit up the night
With a strange cruel light,
In which I saw the heavens
Swallowing hell,
And the earth spawning out
Living death.

I knew that this sun
Was the blood of my people
Gathering in the sky,
Ripping the darkness
With a flaring cry.
For on the highways of the world
It poured along,
In the world's fields
It watered,
The blood knew no rest.
It rose
And split the night's calm.

The Angel of Death
Said to me:
"Thou art my son.
Today I watched thy birth."
And a new heart beat in me

Weak-voiced,
Jerking in agonies of death.
My flesh
Became dead flesh.
The blood flowed dumb
In my veins.

Can I mourn?
I am an elegy.
Lament?
My mind is lamentation.
Can I rise
With death heavy on my limbs,
Or see
When Nothing hangs at my eyelash?
I will mourn and rise.
Your look will ask in my eyes
Atonement for your blood
At the hands of the world
That shed it.

Dahlia Ravikovitch

DISTANT LAND

Tonight, in a sailing boat, I came back
From the isles of the sun, and their coral clusters.
There were girls with combs of gold
Left on the shore in the isles of the sun.

For four years of milk and honey
I roamed the shores on the isles of the sun.
The fruit stalls were heavily laden
And cherries glistened in the sun.

Oarsmen and boatmen from seventy lands
Sailed towards the isles of the sun.
Through four years by shining light
I kept counting ships of gold.

For four years, rounded like apples,
I kept stringing coral beads.
In the isles of the sun merchants and pedlars
Spread out sheets of crimson silk.

And the sea was unfathomable, deeper than any depth,
As I returned from the isles of the sun.
Heavy sundrops, with the weight of honey,
Dripped on the island before sunset.

HARD WINTER

The little berry crackled in the blaze,
And before its splendour vanished it wrapped itself in sadness.
Rain and sun triumphed by turns, and we, in the house,
Were afraid to think of what would happen to us.
The bushes reddened from within, and the pool in hiding:
Everyone set his mind on his own being.
Yet in a moment when my own mind was scattered
I saw how men are uprooted from the world.
Like a lightning stroke on a tree loaded with limbs and tissue,
Their damp branches were trampled like dead grass.
The shutters were cracked, and the walls thin,
And rain and sun kept passing in turn on metal wheels.
All the bodies of plants listened only to themselves.
I did not believe I would survive this time.

Moshe Dor

REVOLUTIONS SPLIT MEN

Madeira, Autumn 1974

Revolutions split men.
Stones stay whole, calm
In their cold completeness, between burnt orchids
With their identity.

From the top of Cabo Giraño, under the umbrella-pines, the
    sea
Attracts to a desirable end. Men are
Split, and can get broken. The endurance of stones
Is not theirs.

Recomeçar . . . Let's start over from the beginning.

OCTOBER 1973

This morning in the circle of the sky strange
Birds pass. Don't hesitate: note seasons
And directions. The circle of the sky
Is ripped this morning by strange
Cries. Don't hesitate: note
Sounds and movements. Strange trees
Reach up this morning to the circle of the sky. Don't
Hesitate: note outline and colouring. Not for days
Will it be inscribed, neither on the sand nor on water,
    how war
Embraces the sky with the thin hands of pain, how
The morning, in clarity, increases despair and hope
In their simplicity. Don't hesitate,
You who compulsively count roots and light-years:
This morning in the circle of the sky strange
Birds pass.

Natan Zach

UNTITLED

All this isn't mine. I reflect
With surprise. Whose, then, is all this?

I don't know. It's a legacy perhaps. No relative
Or kinsfolk have left me anything. Well then?

Perhaps I'll go away from here, if all this is not mine.
Perhaps I'll go away from here, soon.

I don't believe in the honesty of the question.
And I reflect upon myself with surprise.

T. Carmi

STORY

When the woman in the fishing village
Told me of her absent husband
Of the sea that returns every evening to die at her doorstep
I was silent.
I could not say to the shells of her eyes
Your love will return, or
The sea will live again.

(There are days I am unable to find for you
A single word.)

Uzi Shavit

TWO VARIATIONS ON SPRING 1974

1

Blossoms appeared in the land, and
The neglected grapevines climbing in the ruins of Kuneitra
Gave forth fragrance, while
Even the prickles of dead thorns on Mount Hermon
Were unsheathed suddenly, sharp and miraculous, and the
    trails of aircraft
Began sprouting out of soft, white snow, like wounds
Whose bandages have fallen off.

2

How strange that spring is
High in the mountains: no blossom, no voice of the turtle,
A white waste changing slowly
Into a brown waste, and some small birds
Tuning up lightly each morning
Between the fence wires
On the white snow.

Israel Pincas

MEDITERRANEAN

From the hold of this ship
Making for distant places, I
Keep an intent watch.

The waters are taking pity. The evening now
Is like one a thousand years
Ago.

In this old sea of ours
There is no new thing.
Only the wind changes.

I do not think
I have missed anything.
Everything granted since then
Comes as a gift.

A Florentine merchant came
Once, offering
Red glass.
That was in the year
Fourteen hundred
And one.

I had nothing to give
For it, and he sailed away.
Now, I will buy it.

It's like a thousand years ago,
Now, this evening.

Yisrael Hame'iri

IN A PLANE FROM REFIDIM TO LYDDA

I wouldn't have believed it. How the desert suddenly became
distant,
And the dug-in vehicles of destruction grew smaller and
smaller
And the earth began moving slowly, circling as in a dream,
And a strange, icy wind blew, and darkness came slowly
down,
And stars appeared between the clouds, quite clearly stars,
And the heart took off in craziness and wouldn't believe it,
Didn't want to believe it (or perhaps couldn't), and fell
asleep
For a moment, and then came the hard, dry blow of landing.

Original Authors' Names Unknown

MY FATHER'S PRAYER BOOK

My father's prayer book by some miracle
Through many twists of fortune came to me
The prayers in it have all their merits still:
The owner's lost, but it lives uniquely.

The folds are all still in it as before
To mark the prayers he'd not yet spoken through
Wax candle drops witness how things once were
Tears' yellowed circles seal where weeping grew.

The old old book is like an ancient harp
Through all its prayers a bitter weeping flows
Who prays in it can feel a sea's rough grasp
And his soul's forced down by what he does not know.

I AM A DEAD BIRD

I am a dead bird,
A bird that has died,
A bird wrapped in a grey cloak.
I go along and a hooligan mocks me.

Suddenly your stillness surrounds me,
Immortal one.
In the hubbub of the market a dead bird will sing:
You alone endure.
In the hubbub of the market a bird will saunter
With a hidden song.

OTHER POEMS

FOR NO WORDS

My favourite word is loneliness.
It seems to cry out beyond love's lands
To the night's dark wilderness
Where my soul stands
Under an old god's timeless showers
Of love and hate and mysterious bands
Of time dashed down in hours

Where I am changed into nothing
But all my soul I do not know.
And the word that is for loving
Burns cheap below
The hard cold glow
Of my selfish wandering.
Bursting through me it will go
With no wake of wondering.

In you, my dear, all words die
Which I cry alone for comfort
When my dreams and fears are by,
More than a thought
Or a word that is wrought
In a carved vision of night
May our hope in a world, still sought,
Of a wordless season's might.

LOST IN THE SEA

Once in a sand lipped town
On a path above the sea
Where the unfamiliar wind
Lost gull cries in my hair
I walked with a shore bred girl
And told her all my dreams.

My poems leapt to her eyes
As my blood rocked their sound
Far out beyond the sad land
And I knew she listened to
The song that flowed from out
Of her strange sea washed fields.

When night crept in the sky
We turned into her house
Away from the hopeless sea
Where my ghost words flee drowning.
Once we looked back at their nameless grave
And I wept for the love in the town of my heart

A KIND OF PRAYER

Almost silent, I heard, shifting beside me
A ballerina of the slow night street:
Turning, I saw in the dance of the wind
A leaf on its autumn feet.

The dance I have glimpsed in wonder,
Always it seems in retreat.
I dream that its strange choreographer
Knows more than a poet's beat.

UNTITLED

I walk our toy suburb as far as the cigarette machine.
No soul disturbs the flat, amber dusted street,
Except at the far end an amicable train hoots
And shuffles towards night in Birmingham,
Past curtains shielding upstairs bedrooms
And sleek chimneys poised placid in moonlight.

A girl in a white coat clicks by me,
I feel her sudden tremor like a blow;
At a low gate two lovers urgent, fumbling
Move to their last swooping kisses.

A single secular star rides the sky, docile,
As I remember doubt, and wear it – like a gun.

FOR A GIRL BORN IN THE SAME HOUSE ON THE SAME DAY AS ME

This date between us is all
Perhaps we can ever share,
For each year of mine
I lay against your numbered year
Fits badly in its disappointed place.

But if I had not tried to tell
The world myself in words,
And stayed at home like you
And used my words to buy your love
And justified our mothers' obvious partnership

The world in its interested way
Would have approved the precise,
Shaped features of our wedding.
I am not sorry that I broke the pattern;
I'm glad we only share one date.

SIX TOWARDS AFRICA

I
I call out to Africa in the bland night.
It is a wind, a noiseful sea, takes my cry,
Disperses it in a broken continent:

The beloved country, the savage, the unformed,
The faces, like childrens', puzzled into stares,
The nervous because they are maimed.

It is the body of a giant animal, waking
To suffer its strength. It is a poet
Beginning eagerly to sing.

II
Blackness loves the sun, walks in a valley
Of bright shadows, and is vulnerable.

The passion of blackness strokes drums,
Finds movement, is sudden, is urgent.

The need of blackness beats out
Among rough waters, and is human.

III
Tell us, tell us, what will happen
When freedom comes?

When freedom comes
There will be no more apartheid,
No more pass laws
No more beatings
There will be no more starvation
No more lying
No more suspicion
No more murder
When freedom comes
There will be no more apartheid.

And no more hatred
When freedom comes?

When freedom comes there will be growing.

IV
Land is to be loved, not with the marking
Of it, but the caring.

Land is a woman to be loved.

Land is to be drawn in with the hands,
To have the lover's kiss.

Land is a woman to be loved.

Land is neither to be given nor taken in bondage
But freely to know love.

Land is a woman to be loved.

(God cherish the fruit of Africa.)

V
O the white man shall mate with the black woman,
The black man shall mate with the white woman,
The black man shall mate with the black woman
– And none shall be ashamed.

VI
It is not my guilt which calls to you,
Africa, it is my hope. I know
The structures of your pain as well
As one Jew born in Europe in a fiendish age
Can know.
                    I trust your dumbness and your love.

I see a tree planted by streams of waters.

It bears the promised name of Africa.

SACRIFICE

The eyes of the town are silent,
Their prayers are cold,
The victim lies on a knowing altar,
The knife alone is bold.

But when the blood is dripping
Down the altar's side
It lights the eyes in protest
Like a screaming guide.

And the hot sun dries its fingers
As it dries out earth's mud:
The sun is a fearful witness
To the mocking power of blood.

GIFT

In a buttercup field
Among waving clumps
Children played, and lovers
Lay over and under
The blue sky.

And along the lane
Where small stones crunched
I met a girl carrying home
A bunch of yellow flowers
Against her breasts.

I picked another flower
From the green trailing laneside
And handed its small curved tribute
To her gleaming collection.
She smiled endearing in the sun.

UNTITLED

My friend Mustapha is an Arab
He lives in the village
Next to the Kibbutz

Sometimes when work is over
For the day
We meet by the well at the roadside
And eat a felafel together

We talk all kinds of small talk
Until the stars come out
Over Mount Hermon

LEEDS PUB

The little hunchback at the microphone
Paused when her croon broke down
To laugh "O, hell!" at her listeners,
And a young man, tall and husky,
Intoned 'High Noon' with true humility.

My poems lay in a folder flung
Among glasses on the rough table,
And I ached to join the passionate
Procession of singers beside the pianist
Giving out their deep desire for expression;

But though their songs were feebly turned
And wrong, mine were forged for conflicts
They would not comprehend.
At closing time, going up the cobbled street
A wordless singing filled my head.

UNTITLED

Years ago at school, in Glasgow,
I can remember one of those prim Scottish ladies
Who were our teachers, introducing us
To the famous poem of Southey about
How the water comes down at Lodore

Well, that poem stayed with me, more
Than many of more serious import, and
I often remembered that cascade of description
And felt what the rush of water
Must be like, down the hillside.

TO SOME OF MY CONTEMPORARIES

(*On a Volume of Universities Poetry*)

These neatly carved, efficient verses deck
Page after page with their wee, finely canned flourish.
You've certainly had rhetoric by the neck,
And watched uncouth extremes of language perish.

Forgive me, so, if I can see no more
Than skill at underspeaking in your rhymes;
Forgive me if I'd rather you explored
The half-sane edge to living in our times.

A lot of our short past cries out of pain;
Much rough disturbance crawls across the sky:
But "suffering" 's not in fashion, you explain,
Unless governed by the smooth "ironic eye".

Be damned your slick politeness and its tone!
Your sugared confidence you've got the slang -
For sitting on smart whimpers you have sown
's a bloddy great unfathomable bang!

UNTITLED

I met him once, really.
                    He was too religious
For me to talk well to.
                    I was too rough
With his piety,
          too out of terms with his old learning
To meet him much,
                    but still he sensed
I would find my way
                    through the lovingly heaped
Books on his shelves.

UNTITLED

Behind the synagogue was a small room
A place obviously to study in
With a high chair at one end of it

'This (they said) was Rashi's college. Here
The great commentator is supposed to have taught.'
But no-one knows if it was really true
More likely it was just a legend, and Rashi
Never even was in Worms.
                         Though there were
Other Jews living here, till the Nazis came
And destroyed them and
                         all the synagogues.

And then, of course, the Nazis were destroyed
And the new democracy of Germany rebuilt
The synagogue and the legendary room of Rashi
Exactly as it was before.
                    So the myth
Was recreated.

UNTITLED

My love rejects me and my longing for her,
And always runs away from me, it seems;
And not content with that she goes on stealing
My sleep, so I'll not have her in my dreams.

POEM FOR CARMEL

(*Because of her name*)

I remember you a cautious, smiling little girl
Who somehow crossed my bewildered childhood
Before the war and proper fears were sorted out.

The cool whole sound of your name
Remained when you had disappeared
Into your own game of growing, and a red siren-suit
Was the symbol of a delightful lost secret.

Then you emerged again to dance a vision
Of deeper loss around your name,
And I was left with what had grown rarely
Out of the mystery of that one unburied crossing.

Now you have given me two unbroken promises
With the gift of a name that was never requested,
But always kept like children's treasure
Because it sparkles in the sun.

UNTITLED

'The orchard sparkled like a Jew'
Wrote Emily in her verse:
I'm not complaining, understand,
Many have written worse.
But in what way Jews sparkle
For me to say is hard.
Perhaps this very moment
I'm bright as an orchard.

POEM

I never found words for you,
Never in these forms
Placed a syllable
That echoed with your shape.

I have your look,
How always you came to me.
I have movements of you
That warm and chill,

But I could make no catalogue
Of feelings, that would hold
In the very supplest of my lines
What I mean by you.

Be it so:
Your meaning outlives, sustains
These other scarred words
I break about myself.

TWO POEMS OF THE THATCHER ERA

I

Douglas Hurd went up to Brum
To see the pandemonium.

When sticks and stones began to fly
Douglas didn't reason why.

He didn't really want to stay
And policemen hustled him away.

II

Seeing the riots in Peterhead
The Scottish Secretary has said,

It's psychopaths who're doing this,
Which righteous folk will all dismiss.

But it seems to me that sooner or later
Someone should mention Oscar Slater.

UNTITLED

I think it's about time I wrote a sestina
After all one needs from time to time to prove one is a poet
Who takes a reasonable pride in his own craftsmanship
It's all very well to believe in the validity of organic form
But one may too easily soften the contours of the mind
Without a certain structural discipline

For however much one recoils from the suggestion of discipline
And especially the strict complications of a sestina
One cannot wholly deny that a mind
Outleaping itself is what makes or gives birth to a poet
And the constitution of that mind's basic form
Is represented by a somewhat austere craftsmanship

I suppose by this I mean chiefly metrical craftsmanship
For I am aware that though I am lacking in self-discipline
I prize the instinctive manipulation of adjectival form
Which requires skilled metrical sense, and no doubt the sestina
Is the best way in which my kind of poet
Can discover how far metre preserves and shackles his mind

Of course some would dispute this semi-mystical attribute of mind
Believing it all breaks down to assessible craftsmanship
And that the success of even the most transcendental poet
Results from no more than extreme verbal discipline
Let such critics consider how rare is the appearance of a sestina,
Which must surely be their favourite stanzaic form

But then a sestina is not merely a stanzaic form
But the expression of a certain type of mind
Reaching conclusions like the end of line words in the sestina
And justifying them with faith in craftsmanship,
Pretending this is the only real discipline
Necessary to a self-respecting poet

Not that I accept the half-crazy archetypal poet
A sort of dreamy angel stuck in human form
Notoriously unamenable to mundane discipline
Redeemed by the sterile beauty of his mind
And I do not, as I said, despise the demonstration of craftsmanship
Though I shall probably never write another sestina

Nor would I recommend it to any other poet
Who is looking for an original kind of form
Unless they have a masochistic preference for discipline

STATE

Here in my native country
I'm answering for somewhere else.

Exile within exile.
Who's a Jew? Who's a Scot?

What happens after independence?

How much history does anyone need?

What's worth fighting for?

Banal questions posed over and over.

This year in Jerusalem, next year in Edinburgh,
Self – ?

UNTITLED

The Glasgow poet's up there
To show how tough he is.

After all, it's what's expected.

Everybody's heard of Rangers and Celtic, the Gorbals,
Gangs and razor fights.

He's out to show them
What we're made of.

No, son, it'll not do.
Kick harder,
Put the boot in more.

NOTES

NOTES ON PREVIOUSLY COLLECTED POEMS

Pages 14 – 30

PAINTING
Tallis: (Heb.) prayer shawl worn in synagogue by men
Tefilin: (Heb.) phylacteries worn on the arm and forehead by pious Jewish males.

FESTA
Several knowledgeable English Catholics queried the existence of this festival, and suggested Jacobs may have intended Corpus Christi, but Barbara Garvin found a poem by G. Belli entitled Corpus Domini, March 1835, which is about a procession at the Cathedral, San Giovanni in Laterano, in Rome – like this poem. Perhaps the festival only takes place in Italy.
Ascoltaci: (Ital.) Listen to us.
Chuppah: (Heb.) canopy in synagogue used for weddings.

REMOTE ISLAND
In line 20, Jacobs substituted "depopulating" in the 1992 edition of his book for the original (1976) "depopulated".

WHERE
Selach lonu, mechal lonu: (Heb.) from the Yom Kippur liturgy, followed immediately in the poem by the translation. The spelling in this note is a better transliteration than Jacobs'.

DETERRENTS
Heimweh: (Ger.) homesickness.

BOOKSELLERS
Guides for the perplexed: allusion to the famous text by Ben-Maimon, Maimonides, *Guide for the Perplexed*.
Mendele Mokhe Sforim: born White Russia 1835, died Odessa 1917. Classic Yiddish and Hebrew writer.
A.C.Jacobs browsed a lot in bookshops, wherever he travelled. In his last days in Madrid he was a regular visitor to the street of booksellers, *Cuesta Moyano*.

IMMIGRATION
"their hearts were in the east,/ ... no further west": allusion to the

famous line by the greatest Hebrew poet of Spain, Yehuda Halevi, ?1075 - 1141, "My heart is in the east and I am at the edge of the west." (trs. by T. Carmi, *The Penguin Book of Hebrew Verse*).

RETURN
Negev: desert in southern Israel.
"the proper blessing": this phrase was used as the title for A.C. Jacobs' first book. The back cover of the original edition (1976) contains the following text written by Jacobs which remains relevant to his work as a whole:
"There are a great many blessings in Judaism. Usually they praise God for the facts of his creation. Thus, there are blessings to be recited on washing one's hands before eating a meal, on seeing a rainbow, on hearing good or bad news, and many, many more. One is very conscious, if one is brought up in traditional Judaism, of the need to say the appropriate blessing when its situation arises. The poems in this collection are, from one aspect, about living in a world in which there is no certainty about which blessing to say when, or even whether one can bless at all."

OUT
Kol Nidrei: (Heb.) the name and opening words of the service held on the eve of Yom Kippur.
"When it became my task to look through Jacobs' papers this poem began to haunt me. Certainly they were all left 'in drawers among dying papers' and they did 'glow and gnaw' still. Did he mean chuck out the lot or pay the debt and print? 'Whatever one owes them ought to be erased'." [JR]

REGION
Haugh: (Scots.) flat land beside a river

MOVEMENT
The movement was one of the two main western diaspora youth movements, Bnei Akivah, the other being the less religious Habonim. One of Jacobs' group leaders was Chaim Bermant, later to become a novelist. The drive of this ironic poem requires an emphasis on the female leaders.
The *hora* is a lively circular folk-dance.

Pages 36 – 40

SOL

Shlomo ibn Gabirol: 1021/2 (Malaga) - 1055 (Valencia), another great Hebrew poet, "one of several who flourished during the Golden Age of Hebrew poetry in Spain." [ACJ]

El Cambio: the Change (ie from Franco to democracy)

This poem is dated and the place written given. Very rare in Jacobs' work.

ITZIG MANGER BROWSES THROUGH THE PAPERS IN PARADISE

Itzig Manger (the name rhymes with the English 'anger') is one of the most admired and enjoyed Yiddish poets. He was born in 1901 in Czernowitz, Romania. He escaped the German occupation of Paris in World War II to London and later moved to New York. Manger died in Tel Aviv in 1969. His work is characterised by a cunning mixture of simple balladry and dashing literary sophistication. Translations of some of his poems may be found in *The Penguin Book of Modern Yiddish Verse* edited by I. Howe, R. R. Wisse and K. Shmeruk.

Gan Eden: Hebrew and Yiddish term meaning 'the Garden of Eden'. Pronounced, more or less, as in the place name Aden. In this context it means 'heavenly paradise'.

Mechayye: Yiddish word meaning something which gives great pleasure. From Hebrew word meaning literally 'revivifier', so there is a bit of word play here. Pronounced to rhyme approximately with 'messiah'. The 'ch' is pronounced as in Scots 'loch'.

Dovid Hamelech: affectionately, the biblical King David, who was, of course, traditionally regarded as the author and editor of the Psalms. Here again the 'ch' is as in Scots 'loch'.

(Notes to this poem by ACJ in *The Proper Blessing* (expanded edition), 1992.)

Yehuda Halevi: see note to poem 'Immigration'.

NOTES ON UNCOLLECTED POEMS

When the manuscript or typescript has a signature it is indicated in the notes. All other uncollected poems in this book were unsigned. Please note – as described more fully in the introduction – early poems are signed Arthur Jacobs, (on one occasion he signed A. Jacobs); later he used Arthur C. Jacobs, and finally he consistently chose A.C.Jacobs.

Pages 43 – 49

OY

'Oy' is taken from a notebook marked Poems I, containing fifty-five poems certainly written before A.C. Jacobs was seventeen. Notebook II has sixteen poems, none included here. There are about seventy poems in Notebook III, all written by the age of twenty. These include 'A Jew in Glasgow', 'Hydrogen-Bomb Test', 'You', 'Never You', 'Poem in memory...' and the first poem in *The Proper Blessing*, 'Poem for my Grandfather'. The last of these poems was printed in the *Times Literary Supplement*, 5th September 1958.

HYDROGEN-BOMB TEST

Arthur Jacobs 1957

Variant title: *Test*

POEM FOR INNOCENT VICTIMS OF WAR

Arthur Jacobs

ABRAHAM

Arthur Jacobs

Variant:

lines 17/18: *"and"* begins line 18

last line: an allusion to *Mogen Avrohom*, a prayer from the *Shemona Esrei* section, said three times a day.

LANGSIDE

Arthur Jacobs

HAMPSTEAD HEATH: BANK HOLIDAY

Arthur Jacobs

Variants:

line 6: *Voices whirling through fierce rhythms*

line 7: *Are even more fierce;*

THE VICTIM

Arthur Jacobs

Variants:

line 6: *comma after picked*

line 12: *full stop after building*

line 19: *machine!*

line 27: *She, a proud widow is outside your help.*
First printed in *Stand*, 4/1 1960

SOVEREIGN PENNY
Arthur Jacobs
First printed in *Stand* 4/1 1960, without numerals.

THE INFINITE SCALE
Arthur Jacobs

POEM FOR JOHN KNOX
Arthur Jacobs
Variants:
line 1: *greasy*
line 6: *whipped*
(see also note to Philip Hobsbaum's essay, p.225)
burd: (Scots) maiden (obs.). 'Burd Helen' occurs in an early 18th century Scottish ballad, 'Helen of Kirkconnel'.
Printed in *Stand*, as above.

VERSES OF ANXIETY
Arthur Jacobs
Variants:
line 5: *may blow us*
line 11: *They are worried by this at respectable conferences*
line 12: *at all.*
Printed in *Jewish Quarterly* Summer 1958

POEM IN MEMORY. . .
Arthur Jacobs
Variants:
II:
line 1: *no comma*
III:
line 8: *[for fatherland] fatherhood.* This could be a strange typographical error printed as such in *The Jewish Quarterly*.
line 13: *[for thrown] drawn*

Pages 54 – 60

III:
dropping lines *21 & 22*
This early poem written around 1957 was surely inspired by the novel *House of Dolls* by Katsetnik 135633 which was first published in English in 1956. Jacobs' sister informs us that both she and Arthur read the book at that time.
Printed in *Jewish Quarterly* Summer 1958

NEVER YOU
Arthur Jacobs

OLD LADY
Arthur Jacobs

THROUGH THE DARK HOUSE . . .
Arthur Jacobs

ON A TRIP TO YORK
Arthur Jacobs
Variant:
Sub-title: *terrible massacre*
We thought, not unreasonably, that Arthur's poem, first published in Jon Silkin's *Stand*, might have been influenced by Silkin's famous and powerful poem about the Jews of York but Silkin tells us that it was the other way round. "Arthur's poem was exemplary. It taught me that one man's courage could influence another's . . . And, indeed, some Christians were offended later on when they heard me read my poem in public".

ALIEN POEM
Arthur Jacobs
Variant:
line 15: .... *is a better promise.*

THE ANARCHIST
Arthur Jacobs
In an early notebook Jacobs, aged about seventeen, states he has stopped propagandising for anarchism.

TOWARDS A GRIEF
Arthur Jacobs
Variant title: *My Love, in Sorrow*

YOU
Arthur Jacobs

POEM TO A SICK WOMAN
Arthur Jacobs

AGAINST THE IDEOLOGIES
Arthur Jacobs

A GLOSS ON TALMUD
Arthur Jacobs

RECORD OF A WALK HOME
Arthur Jacobs

'INTRODUCTION TO A SCOTTISH SEQUENCE'
Arthur Jacobs
Variant:
3rd stanza subdivided into 3 stanzas of 6, 2, 2 lines
It is not possible to establish what the sequence might have eventually consisted of, apart from 'Interlude' which follows immediately.

INTERLUDE
Variant:
lines 4/5 :
Is standing fixedly beside me.
I think in a moment he is going to ask me to leave
The motto of the city is 'Let Glasgow Flourish'.

PARTY AT DOONFOOT
Scaur: (Scots) cliff
Arthur Jacobs

Pages 69 – 77

POEM
'I am a tall talmudic Jew'
Arthur Jacobs

A JOKE ACROSS THE NORTH SEA
Arthur Jacobs

THE DEPARTURE
Arthur Jacobs

I CHOOSE NEITHER . . .
Arthur Jacobs
First line: see note to poem 'Immigration' in previous section.

IN EARLY SPRING
Arthur Jacobs
Variant:
stanza 7, line 3: *My friend the live Silkin*

THE ASTROLOGER
Arthur Jacobs
This description fits the astrologer Ernest Page who frequented the Soho coffee houses in the 1950s, and charged three shillings and sixpence for a consultation.

O, ENGLAND
Arthur Jacobs
Published in *The Jewish Chronicle,* February 24 1995

JANUARY POEM
Variants:
Dedication: *for Joan*
line 1: *Snow, love . . .*
line 5, *two variants: unstrung, unstung*

MOSAIC
Variant:
line 5: *. . . knowing*

Pages 78 – 89

UNTITLED
'Snapshots, mementoes of the glaring sun'
A. Jacobs

OLD THEME
Sambatyon: legendary river found in the Aggada (that part of rabbinic literature not dealing with legal matters. See the famous collections by Ginzberg, Agnon, etc.).
Lost tribes: the ten tribes of Israel taken away by the invading Assyrians in 720 BC.

ON A BALKAN VISA
Variants:
Title: *On a Transit Visa*
line 9: *like an empty slime*

NOTES FOR URIEL DA COSTA
The eponymous subject of the poem was a famous Jewish freethinker. He was born in Oporto in 1585 and committed suicide in Amsterdam in 1640. He had been excommunicated twice and publicly lashed in the synagogue. Some authorities think his theological writings might have influenced a later and greater writer, Baruch Spinoza. Da Costa's life is well worth exploring. Among works of literature about him is Charles Reznikoff's verse play, *Uriel Acosta* (in *Nine Plays*, 1927).

UNTITLED
'Lately up in the Lake District'
The original poem is by Robert Southey. Its title is 'The Cataract of Lodore' subtitled 'Described in Rhymes for the Nursery'.

> And to hear how the water
> Comes down at Lodore,
> With its rush and its roar.

See also earlier poem, 'Years ago at school in Glasgow' (p.182)

UNTITLED
'Up there in Wordsworthshire, on a warm spring evening,'
Manuscript evidence suggests Jacobs was still working on the first stanza.

Pages 90 – 94

DR ZAMENHOF
Arthur C. Jacobs
The Esperanto words mean "We do not speak Esperanto", which is obviously an ironic joke. This poem concludes with a very complex and multi-layered gloss on the relationship between the first language of half the victims, the language of the perpetrators and the doomed world language invented by the pre-Holocaust Polish Jew who lived in the land where the Germans sited the death camps; but ACJ has made a mistake in the Esperanto, possibly unintentionally. The word "la" should not be there.

PAINTER
Arthur C. Jacobs

SABBATH MORNING: MEA SHEARIM and **RELIGIOUS QUARTER** (see p. 98)
Arthur C. Jacobs
Mea Shearim: just outside the Old City, this is home to the most orthoprax Jews in Jerusalem. The feel of the quarter is that of an East European *shtetl.*

SAMSON
Arthur C. Jacobs
Variants:
line 10: . . . *in his own* ....."
line 15: *two variants:*
But the final act
But the extreme will
Printed in *Jerusalem Post*

MENORAH
Arthur C. Jacobs
Jerusalem 1960

TO A TEACHER OF HEBREW LITERATURE
Arthur C. Jacobs

OVER THERE, JUST HERE
Arthur C. Jacobs

BAB EL-WAD
"At Bab el-Wad on the road to Jerusalem trucks blown up in the first Israel-Arab war were left exactly as they were when it happened. Also, on the road are memorial forests to martyrs destroyed in the Second World War by the Germans." [Note by ACJ.] Many of the trees (line 8) were destroyed in the recent fire, July 95.

BY KIRYAT SHEMONA
Arthur C. Jacobs
Kiryat Shemona: a town in northern Israel.

ISRAELI ARAB
Variant:
line 10: '. . . . we never seek'

LOVE IN THIS BITTER SEASON
Arthur C. Jacobs

FOR THE ANGLO-SAXON POETS
"Anglo-Saxon" is used in Israel as a synonym for Anglophone. This certainly amused Jacobs. The dedicatees are well known English-language poets living in Jerusalem.

AFTERWARDS
Variant:
line 10: *no comma*

PORTRAIT
Arthur C. Jacobs
Variants:
line 10: *comma*
line 12: *no comma*

EARTHQUAKE
Arthur C. Jacobs

PERHAPS . . .
Arthur C. Jacobs

Pages 103 – 110

PATTERNS OF CULTURE
Variant sub-title: *(An allusion to the book of Ruth Benedict)*

HILLS
A.C.Jacobs
Variants :
Title: *Judean Hills*
lines 7/8/9:
This is a country where miracles
Were in repute. An extraordinary flash
Met...

CLASSIC
A.C.Jacobs
first published in *The Jewish Chronicle*, June 9, 1978

CRISIS
A.C.Jacobs
Variant:
no dedicatee.

HERE
First published in *The Jewish Chronicle,* February 24, 1995

TONGUE
A.C.Jacobs
Written in the Glasgow dialect.

UNTITLED
'Among these green hills'
Variant:
line 10: *Whose images touched me* or *Whose images moved me*

WHAT ARE YOU TALKING ABOUT?
A.C.Jacobs
Variant:
line 11: *in England now*
First published in *Acumen*, 18, October 1993.

PLACE
A.C.Jacobs

DEAR MR LEONARD
Variant Title: *For the Makers*
Mr Leonard: the poet Tom Leonard, some of whose poems are written in Glasgow vernacular.
This poem is interesting from a multilingual point of view because the aunt uses two Yiddish words and one Scots word (see below) while speaking English probably with a mixture of Yiddish accent and local Glasgow accent.
froom: religious
trayfi: non-kosher
scunners: upsets

IN EDINBURGH AGAIN
Printed in *The Scottish Review*, 10, 1978.

ISOLATION
The Scottish Review, as above.

EDINBURGH NEW TOWN
Variants:
line 3: *I passed. . .*
line 6: *I was*
line 9: *Or I read it*
line 10: *(it was), was it not*
line 12: *Back through my childhood, in those spaced out suburbs*
line 13: *That brought lives together, and drove them apart*
Leerie turns out to be the Scots word for lamplighter. Young readers of the poem outside Scotland could be forgiven for thinking it was the lamplighter's name.

HÖLDERLIN
This mysterious and beautiful fragment reads like a translation from Hölderlin but is clearly a poet's homage to the greatest of German poets. "Tower" could also allude to Rilke, Yeats and Joyce.

Pages 114 – 120

REPORT
Variants:
Title: *Untitled*
line 5: *In disputed territory*
line 13: *like all of us*
Lines 9 and 10 contain an ironic allusion to a famous poem of Auden, line 11 ditto to the title of Empson's first book.
Line 5: "Land of Israel" and "Palestine" translate each other in Hebrew and Arabic respectively and also bear the political weight of the variant above. Jacobs was acutely aware of the problem.

TRIOLET
A.C.Jacobs used to read his poems at Torriano Meeting House in Kentish Town at the Sunday evenings organised by poet and publisher (and co-editor of this book) John Rety.

All the poems from here on were found in ACJ's notebooks in Madrid.

ROMANCE
"The film referred to is ¡Ay Carmela! directed by Carlos Saura." [Note by ACJ]

IN MADRID
"The poem mentioned is a famous one by by Gustavo Adolfo Bécquer (1836 - 1870) beginning 'Volverán las oscuras golondrinas'." [Note by ACJ]

1492
A.C.Jacobs
The year the Jews were expelled from Spain, and Columbus (possibly a descendant of Jews who converted to Catholicism after the massacres a century earlier) arrived in America.

CUTTING DOWN
Although found in Madrid, this may have been written earlier.

READINGS
A.C.Jacobs

LOVE POEM
Line one begins like a traditional blessing (see note to the poem 'Return') but personalises it in a religiously incorrect way.
Line two alludes to a prayer in the liturgy.

UNTITLED
'All poets are Jews,'
Variant:
line 4: *Of the falsely virtuous*

ETHICS
The quote is a celebrated statement by the great and much loved Rabbi Hillel (conjecturally the teacher of Jesus), as reported in "Ethics of the Fathers" in the Talmud. The quote, in part or in entirety, has been used by many authors, eg by Primo Levi as the title of his novel *If not now, when?*

NOTES ON TRANSLATIONS

GENERAL NOTE ON THE TRANSLATIONS

As with two previous Menard translators who died before publication, Masha Enzensberger and Jonathan Griffin (see publisher's note appended to her translation of Mandelstam's *A Necklace of Bees*, Menard/Kings 1992 and to his translation of Pessoa's *Message*, Menard/ Kings 1992), it was sadly not possible to discuss the final versions of Arthur Jacobs' translations with our friend and author. I therefore decided to go through the translations with Hebrew expert Risa Domb – for whose help I am very grateful – and we dropped completely four Vogel translations as well as translations of a number of other poets: these translations contained what were very clearly unintended mistakes, as opposed to intended "mistakes", ie that area of licence where a translator poet who knows the original language well, as Arthur did, makes changes in one register in order to obtain a compensation in another, in the holistic interests of that coalition of dialectically interacting registers we call a completed poem or that special kind of poem we call a poem in translation.

In a number of cases of very minor unintended mistakes, as pointed out by Risa Domb, I made a few minimal changes in Arthur's words – as I did in Masha's and Jonathan's, see above – adhering as closely as I could to his tone and general approach. I am aware that some people including Arthur himself might disapprove, but with translations, even such beautiful ones as many of Arthur's translations are, I believe we are dealing with an ontologically different artefact from original poems – hence the apparatus of variants in the Uncollected Poems section of this book, where the editors have chosen what they read as the best variant (not necessarily the latest one or published one) for the text, and listed the others in the notes. Space does not permit an equivalent treatment of the translations.

When going through the papers of A.C. Jacobs we recognised two or three poems as definitely being translations although there was no indication of the author of the original text. This alerted us to the possibility that there might be more. We identified about twenty candidates – they *sounded* like translations – and discussed the problem with Risa Domb, who identified a few more. Of the remaining texts we decided, in the end, that most of them were Jacobs' own work (should any reader identify other translations among his own *Uncollected Poems* we would be most grateful though not particularly mortified) – but two poems stubbornly insisted on sounding like translations. If any reader can confirm that either of these poems *is* a translation we would be most grateful and, indeed, feel vindicated. AR.

NOTES ON THE POETS TRANSLATED

One day it may be possible to publish a wider selection of A.C.Jacobs' translations, with a commentary on his approach to the originals and the relationship of his work as a translator to his work as an original poet: "your northern Anglo-Scottish pragmatical self coming down hard on your more emotional Jewish self" (letter from Dan Jacobson to Jacobs) is a reference to and an excellent description of a typical, indeed fundamental, movement within many poems of Jacobs but also, accidentally, serves to describe the pressures on this particular poet when engaging in the complex process of negotiation we call the translation of poetry, especially – for him – Hebrew poetry, written both in Israel and the Diaspora. In a note appended to his pamphlet *A Bit of Dialect*, Jacobs is quoted as saying that the cultural schism he inherited has made him "particularly aware of dying and revived languages and the tensions between languages and dialects and similar matters." For the time being, the following notes are appended as an interim guide for the reader with not too much knowledge of the Hebrew poets included.

DAVID VOGEL

David Vogel was born in Satanov, Podolya, South-west Russia, in 1891 and, most likely, died in a concentration camp after being arrested by the Nazis in France in 1944. He spent a year in Palestine in 1929 but returned to Europe. He wrote in Hebrew (and Yiddish) and is now commonly regarded as an important forerunner of Hebrew modernism. Readers are referred to the entry on him in the *Encyclopaedia Judaica* by his editor, the well known Hebrew poet (and Menard author), Dan Pagis. The out of print Menard edition of Vogel contains a long introduction by A.C.Jacobs, not reprinted here.

AVRAHAM BEN-YITZHAK

Avraham Ben-Yitzhak (Avraham Sonne) was born in Przemysl, East Galicia (now West Ukraine) in 1883 and died in Israel in 1950, having settled in Palestine in 1938. As stated in the acknowledgements, Ben-Yitzhak published only eleven poems in his lifetime (perhaps two thirds of his output), yet he, like Vogel, is regarded as an important forerunner of later trends. Most of the eleven poems were written before World War One and are among the very earliest poems whose rhythms presuppose the Sephardi pronunciation of modern Hebrew. He was very influential on a personal level – Canetti, for example, regarded him as a mentor and the feelings of Leah Goldberg (perhaps Israel's greatest woman poet) for him as a man and as a poet were well known. Her essay on Ben-Yitzhak, often quoted by T.Carmi, deserves to be translated. It contains the following sentence: "He was the first Hebrew poet whose watch displayed not merely the specific Jewish time, but rather the time kept by world literature at the same hour." The personal note about the poet which Jacobs had nearly completed before he died was inserted looseleaf in the limited edition published by Tim Gee Editions, and is reprinted here.

HAYYIM NAHMAN BIALIK

Bialik was born near Zhitomir, Ukraine, in 1873 and died in Tel Aviv in 1934. His stature and influence as a poet is homologous to that of Agnon as a prose writer. Though he was undoubtedly the major Hebew poet emanating from the late nineteenth century Hebrew revival in Eastern Europe and was, indeed, the most important Hebrew poet since the great Spanish figures centuries earlier, this did not prevent him being "dethroned" by Shlonsky, Alterman and other modernist poets of the Second Aliyah (wave of immigration) in the twenties, who in their turn were dethroned by Zach, Amichai and others later on. His early intellectual mentor was the towering figure of Ahad Ha'am in Odessa. There Bialik was also close to Mendele (see Jacobs poem `Booksellers') and the historian Dubnow. After periods in Warsaw and Berlin he arrived in Tel Aviv in 1924. Ruth Nevo's translation of *Selected Poems* of Bialik was published by Dvir in Israel in 1981.

YEHUDA AMICHAI

Born in Wurzburg in Germany in 1924, and arrived in Palestine with his family in 1936. Amichai, widely regarded as the most important living Hebrew poet, is well known to English readers – thanks to several volumes of translations (Menard published one in 1977) and also to personal appearances at poetry festivals. He fought in the British Army's Jewish Brigade in World War Two and later in the Israeli War of Independence.

A.L.STRAUSS

A.L.Strauss was born in Aachen in 1892, arrived in Palestine in 1935, and died in Jerusalem in 1953. This is the only translation of a poem by him we have ever seen.

DAHLIA RAVIKOVITCH

Born in Tel Aviv in 1936. One of the most admired and influential poets of her generation, she has also translated Yeats and Eliot. She is from the first generation of Hebrew poets to be influenced by "Anglo-Saxon" (see Jacobs' poem 'For the Anglo-Saxon Poets') rather than German, Russian or French models. Menard published Chana Bloch's selection in 1978.

MOSHE DOR

Born in 1932 in Tel Aviv, Dor has been an influential figure, not only as a a poet, but as editor, translator, journalist, and was one of a distinguished series of writers who served as cultural attache in London. His correspondence with the obstinately purist translator A.C.Jacobs is a model of diplomacy. Like Zach, Dor's use of syntax is particularly subtle. See the selected poems published by Menard in 1978.

NATAN ZACH

Natan Zach was born in Berlin in 1930, arriving in Haifa in 1936, the same year Amichai arrived in Jerusalem. He is Professor of Comparative Literature at Haifa University but it is as a poet that his influence has made itself felt, and he has been widely translated. His stripped down, anti-rhetorical verse, influenced by imagism on the one hand and certain East European poets on the other, translates well into English (when well done), as does Amichai's poetry – albeit for different reasons.

T. CARMI

T. Carmi was born Carmi Tcharny in New York in 1925 into a religious family where Hebrew was spoken. He arrived in Jerusalem in 1947. Along with Amichai and Zach he is certainly the best known

Hebrew poet of our time. His work relies less on imagery than Amichai's, less on syntax than Zach, but is rich and complex in its diction, incorporating ancient motifs in contemporary idiom. He died in 1994.

UZI SHAVIT

Professor of Hebrew literature at the University of Tel Aviv, member of Kibbutz Sedot Yam and chairman of Kibbutz Hameuchad Publishing House. This may be the first translation of any text of his into English.

ISRAEL PINCAS

Pincas was born in Sofia, Bulgaria in 1935, arriving in Tel Aviv in 1944. Very little of his work has been translated, perhaps only this poem.

YISRAEL HAME'IRI

Born on Kibbutz Givat Haim in 1948. Better known as a prose writer. This may be the first translation of any text of his into English.

Pages 147 – 170

A.R.Ben-Yitzhak
BLESSED ARE THOSE WHO SOW AND DO NOT REAP

The title and first line of this poem evokes and reverses the meaning of Psalm 126 verse 5 and Isaiah 30 verse 20. By translating the repeated Hebrew word *ashrei* as 'blessed' rather than the more expected 'happy' Jacobs evokes, surely on purpose, the Beatitudes in the Sermon on the Mount (Matthew Chapter 5, 3 - 11). The Hebrew of Ben-Yitzhak does not allude to the Hebrew texts underlying the Beatitudes.

The last line of the poem, the eleventh and final poem published in the poet's lifetime, has been read as an allusion to his own silence. Whether – as Allen Tate said of John Peale Bishop's silence – the poet heard the phone ringing and did not answer or did not hear the phone ringing or the phone did not ring at all, remains a matter for speculation.

Bialik
ON YOUR DESOLATE HEARTS
Mezuzah: extract from the Torah in a container fastened at an angle to the right doorpost of Jewish houses as a symbolic reminder of devotion and piety. In folk tradition, an amulet to ward off evil.
Shamash: synagogue beadle

Amichai
JERUSALEM 1967
Israel had occupied the old city in the six day war a few months previously.

Dor
OCTOBER 1973
This was the month of the Yom Kippur War.

Shavit
TWO VARIATIONS ON SPRING 1974
Kuneitra: on the Golan Heights
Mount Hermon: part of a range in Lebanon, Syria and Israeli occupied territory.

NOTES ON OTHER POEMS

Pages 175 – 182

FOR NO WORDS
Arthur Jacobs

LOST IN THE SEA
One of only two 'figured' poems in Jacobs' work.
Arthur Jacobs

A KIND OF PRAYER
Arthur Jacobs

UNTITLED
'I walk our toy suburb as far as the cigarette machine.'
Arthur Jacobs

FOR A GIRL BORN IN THE SAME HOUSE ON THE SAME DAY AS ME
Arthur Jacobs

SIX TOWARDS AFRICA
Arthur Jacobs

SACRIFICE
Arthur Jacobs

GIFT
Variant Title: *Prelude*
Arthur Jacobs

LEEDS PUB
Arthur Jacobs

UNTITLED
'Years ago at School in Glasgow'
See last note on p. 201

TO SOME OF MY CONTEMPORARIES (ON A VOLUME OF UNIVERSITIES POETRY)

Arthur Jacobs

Universities Poetry was an annual which came out for several years. It would be amusing if tactless to try to figure out which volume is referred to, and who the editors were.

The use of "wee" and "bloddy" is a reminder that A.C. Jacobs spoke English with a pronounced Glasgow (Scots) accent and this should be taken into consideration if reading his poems aloud.

UNTITLED

'The orchard sparkled like a Jew'

This is a line from Emily Dickinson's "The day came slow – till Five o'clock" (1862), poem 304 (p. 143) in *The Complete Poems of Emily Dickinson* (ed. T.H. Johnson) Faber and Faber 1970.

TWO POEMS OF THE THATCHER ERA

1. The poem was presumably written some time between 1985 and 1989, when Douglas Hurd was Home Secretary.

   Brum: Birmingham

2. Oscar Slater: a Jew at the centre of a famous Glasgow murder trial – taken up by Conan Doyle – early in the century. He was, according to Chaim Bermant (personal communication), "a shyster but not a murderer".

STATE

A.C.Jacobs

line 9: The Passover story, told each year, contains the famous invocation "Next year in Jerusalem!"

Published in *The Jewish Chronicle*, June 1979.

UNTITLED

'The Glasgow poet's up there'

Rangers and Celtic are the two major soccer teams in Glasgow, with Protestant and Catholic supporters respectively. Perhaps Jacobs was neutral.

ESSAYS

Philip Hobsbaum
Frederick Grubb
John Rety
Anthony Rudolf

A.C.JACOBS – A PERSONAL MEMOIR
Philip Hobsbaum

Arthur Jacobs told me that he belonged to an orthodox Jewish family resident in the Gorbals, a then notorious slum south of the Clyde in Glasgow. Most of what I knew about Arthur came from his own lips. As a young man, for example, he said that his writing was mostly in Yiddish, though I never saw any specimens of this. He also said that he was in the printing trade. All this was told me in a soft Scottish voice, decidedly unlike the guttural blare I associate with the Empire's second city.

I met Arthur forty years ago at the Ben Uri Art Gallery in London. He was a constant frequenter of literary gatherings, a shy man on the edge of an audience. Somehow or other Arthur got round to telling me that he wrote verse. Operating on a hunch that the verse might be worth reading, I asked him to come along to a weekly gathering of poets that met in my flat in Kendal Street, off the Edgware Road.

There Arthur got to know Edward Lucie-Smith, Peter Porter, Peter Redgrove and George MacBeth, all of whom in 1955 had yet to make their names. Arthur's work was, and remained, intensely Jewish in subject matter and method, and naturally attracted especial attention from the various Jews who came along to the Group. As well as myself, these were my then fiancée, Hannah Kelly; also Rosemary Joseph and Rachel Keller, both of whom I had met at the Ben Uri; together with Jon Silkin. Jon was not a regular member but an occasional and welcome visitor. He published some of Arthur's early poems in his influential magazine, *Stand.*

Reserved, and even taciturn, though Arthur was, he had a way of making himself felt. His poems were singularly well adapted to his voice, and his voice to his poems: quiet, sombre, yet somehow resonant. In all, three separate meetings of the Group were set aside for the reading and subsequent discussion of Arthur's work. The first reading included two or three poems from a sequence concerned with his grandfather.

One referred to the *Yahrzeit* (annual memorial) ritual:

> Today, a candle in a glass
> Burns slowly on the mantelpiece.
> Wheesht, the dead are here.

Characteristically in this poem, the Jewish and the Scottish elements are fused. Another was more adverse, connecting his grandfather with John Knox:

> A greasy rigid Puritan, *
> You were most of the landscape.

Yet a third refers to a custom that had grown up, whereby a grandfather presented his grandson as a memento of his barmitzvah with a gold sovereign:

> I know what he wants:
> To be a proud charm on a string round my neck.
> When I tug at him for luck or breath
> I'll choke.

It is poignant to consider that Arthur was a lifelong asthmatic. His Jewish heritage could not be got rid of, any more than his Scottishness, but it sometimes lay heavily on his chest.

On another occasion, the Group heard a poem, on an ambitious scale for Arthur, "In Memory of all the Jewish Girls who were made Prostitutes for German Soldiers and then suffered the Ultimate Martyrdom." It is written, with dark and deliberate irony, in the manner of the Song of Solomon:

> My sister is dumb in the hands of her spoilers.
> The eyes of my bride stare at those who will rape her.

This is a difficult subject, and it says a lot for Arthur's technique, as well as his sincerity, that he was able to succeed in his endeavour. His coevals listened to him with respect.

All these poems, and several others, date from the 1950s, when I knew Arthur best. In the early 1960s he went to Israel, where he lived for three years and became an accomplished translator of such poets as Avraham Ben-Yitzhak and David Vogel. By the time he returned, I had left London, and our subsequent meetings were occasional and by chance, at this or that literary gathering. The last time I saw him was in 1973, at a poetry recital on the Edinburgh Festival fringe. But we kept, intermittently, in touch by letter.

Some of his later verse was about Spain, a country where he sojourned when he was not in London, though I believe that London was his usual domicile. It is a matter of regret that our friendship, such as it was, ended in acrimonious correspondence. This was not long before he died.

I had started a magazine called *The Glasgow Review* backed by the university where I still work. Arthur had written to me about something else, but I asked him, as a poet native to Glasgow, if my co-editors and myself could consider some of his recent verse for publication. The pieces that he sent me proved to be very slight, rather like scribblings on the backs of picture post-cards. Even if I had seen my way to printing them, my co-editors certainly would not have concurred. The pieces had to be returned. Arthur took what he saw as a wholesale rejection very personally. He accused me of having sold out to careerism! If that had been true, I would hardly have asked for sight of his poems in the first place, and certainly would not be writing about their author now.

Of course, I did not – did anyone? – expect his sudden death. My obituary in The Guardian, May 5 1994, was an attempt to make partial amends. He must have aged, but I still remember him as the solitary, soft-spoken man who used to haunt the fringes of the literary scene in London. For me, his epitaph is not in the Mourner's Kaddish or the Book of Job, but rather in one of his own poems, 'For No Words'. Was it ever published? It begins:

> My favourite word is loneliness.
> It seems to cry out beyond love's lands
> To the night's dark wilderness.

* Jacobs later changed "greasy" to "goading" (see p.52). Hobsbaum is quoting the Group's privately circulated broadsheet.

THE WIDEAWAKE STRANGER

Frederick Grubb

All the poems not collected,
That are left lying in drawers
Among dying papers, or go roaming
On pages one can't recall,
Which of them really exist
And which are imagined?

Whatever one owes them ought
To be erased.[1]

In what spirit do we take this? When A.C.Jacobs died in Madrid in 1994, he was thought to have been an unprolific poet. It was then found he'd left nearly 200 poems in various stages of typing, handwriting, though not it seems computering. For one who wished "to keep close/To the unsayable" he knew that

There is deliberate silencing,
To speak up against it
To make oneself heard.[2]

As readers we must find our own titles for his untitled poems. A few are drafts, fragments, sketches, literary exercises, echoic or immature. Naming the poems, searching them as they search us, we realise this wideawake stranger (a phrase originally used of Bernard Spencer)[1] was a loner with a striking range of friends, forms, and subjects. Exploring the poems, we recreate ACJ's many moods, tones, languages, humours, anxieties, conflicts, rebellions, conformisms (not often), angers, loves, roots, and uproots, the best poems shining in that clear outline and open space – like free-standing sculpture – the reader makes for them. For with range, Jacobs has the gift of immediacy: moving and on the move, between place and place, exile and homecoming, ghetto and diaspora, active and contemplative, presence and absence, he finds you and speaks to you directly:

Oh, well, look,
This is a poem for you.
You know who I mean.[3]

It may be true, as Anthony Rudolf has suggested, that Jacobs is the Anglo-Jewish poet becoming more Jewish as he grows older "notwithstanding alienation from institutional Judaism as described in his celebrated poem 'Where'". It is also true that he has that Scots-Jewish accent "heard in zany poems of Ivor Cutler" and in ACJ's social-realist epigrams given to cursing, flyting, parodying, and questioning, whether of Glasgow Poets, Leeds Pubs, or Douglas Hurds. Primarily, he was a citizen of the world, if worried about his passport (see 'Travelling Abroad'); also, perhaps, the last of the autodidacts in the sense of free of both Academic Eng Lit – as Philip Hobsbaum points out – and freelance cliques too. In 'To Some of my Contemporaries', on a Movement influenced anthology, he mocks the "slick politeness" of "underspeakers" for whom " "suffering"'s not in fashion, you explain/Unless governed by the smooth "ironic eye" ". To this he replies in McDiarmidian tones and just a slap at Eliot that "For sitting on smart whimpers you have sown/'s a bloddy great unfathomable bang!". To a Southern ear, when in Wordsworthshire a barlady kicks hikers out of a posh hotel in a dry central lowland voice – "Ah'm sorry lads/But yull no' get served here" those tones echo still

Reflecting, I suppose, the poet in his long later phase
Of settled gentility. But I, in keeping with most modern
scholars

Am stirred by the decade or so of poems that plunge
Into obstinate questionings, of vagrants and the like.[4]

Other voices: the poet hears "the poet Heine calling to Scotland/Across the cold, liberating waves". Here the full title is needed: 'A Joke Across the North Sea'. Holidaymakers at Ayr "eat up the beach with cries". He is heard praying to a God he doubts, but praying, no thanks to Freud:

Descend neither in Kirk nor synagogue
Nor university nor pub.
But on a handy summit like Ben Lomond
Make me a new Sinai, and please God
Can we have less of the thou-shalt-not?[5]

He argues with Knox – "I, sinning against my grandfather's messiah . . . Remember and am consoled/By burd Helen and the loves of Robert Burns" ('Poem for John Knox', a hefty title), fears being kicked out of Glasgow Art Gallery ("I stare down at the beauty of Kelvingrove") for not looking at the pictures, feels in Langside that "the summit, half proud, inhales/ The air of battle". Between East and West, he chooses neither:

For I am shaped by the North
And my history reaches down through old maps
Of Europe, and jumbled alphabets meaning . . . [6]

What calls him north he does not know entirely:

Not a piper on a rock
Dirling hypnotic music through my sky,
Nor lust for whisky washed down with strong ale
Against a foggy background of bare hills,
Nor Raeburn's beauties near ethereal
(With jeans and shorter hairstyles, nowadays)
Made me leave her in the south
Who was cool and English [7]

Down in Golders Green you see

Small symptoms of alienation
among its well-fed residents.
Candles on Friday,
a beard or two, an occasional
Joke in Yiddish . . .
. . . .

There are one or two signs
of otherness.
Still, don't worry.
They scarcely jar. [8]

To which 'N.W.2.: Spring' is a witty pastoral foil. A sense of dislocation will disturb ACJ at any time, in Princes Street maybe "that song is anti-Scottish/Though she can't remember exactly what/It says about us. God save the Queen", being lost in the Home Counties, "One of the girls made a joke about it/About us outside the ghetto . . . Only a joke, of course", in Edinburgh when the lamps are lit early

> A most Stevensonian evening (was it not?)
> As we walked along the pavement of that fine terrace,
> Back through our childhoods, in those suburbs
> That brought us together, and drove us apart. [9]

Behind or within or beyond all this is Jacobs' finest poem, silence filled by a primal word, the biblical breath or spirit of God "moving after creation"

> But nothing follows:
> No other words
> Cross the darkness outside.
> There is only *ruach*,
> The word for the sound of the wind. [10]

In Jerusalem, this is felt as inwardness, in the refrain "call in your soul", against the brashness of Tel Aviv, a city "Dazzled by the glare of brutal public signs . . . Yet the name still holds a legend/Peopled by the pride of a rebirth". As for York, scene of a massacre in 1190, it has its own message:

> And in the Minster, where
> The good archbishops gently smile in stone,
> I want to scream in Hebrew . . .
> But I stand and watch the choirboys, two by two,
> In red and white, marching to evensong.[11]

On the rare occasions when you met Arthur at all, usually in the road, pub, or café, "at a slight angle to the universe", he would take up bits of conversation broken off years before, leaving you oblivious of people met weekly or monthly who talked a lot more. It was the same continuity in the poems, whose characteristic style is neither free verse nor conventional forms, apart from a few epigrams, lyrics, burlesques and other rimings, betimes contumacious. His best riming poem is the Itzig Manger quatrains, vintage self-irony in a quite new voice, with delightful anti-pedantic Notes to end notes (we hope):

Manger sits in *Gan Eden*
Drinking a glass of tea.
The "Heavenly Literary Supplement",
In Yiddish, is on his knee . . .

And then he sees a translation
Of a poem written by me.
A.C.Jacobs, he murmurs,
Now who on earth could he be? [12]

"Oy, is this a poem" says Manger (died 1969, balladist and scholar) imagining a poem by earthling Jacobs translated into Yiddish. "Funny exclamation/Almost as if it were born in another climate" ACJ had written in an early British poem, 'Oy'. A good review of Manger having appeared, the Notes assure us that 'mechaye' in Yiddish means 'pleasure', in Hebrew 'revivifier' (Joycean epiphany, maybe?), it rhymes with 'messiah' and is pronounced as Scots 'loch'. As the poem ranges and jokes, a world of wit opens up, earning ACJ a generous fee in God's Oxford Anthology. We hope.

A contrary use of a naïf rime scheme for the violent facts gives a strange piquancy to 'Lesson Number 24', about gun-toting in an unnamed country which could be – where? It recalls Auden's 'A Shock' ("frisked by a cop for weapons."). Other poems are plain realism, scarcely pentametric, rather unpsalmic, just adding up facts, like his 'Kibbutz' "halfway up a slope/Are the green frail huts of a settlement/Where some are trying to establish absolute/Equality, necessary kinds of links". As with Manger's "Oy, is this a poem" the effect is of sharp double-edged suggestiveness; poem or not, equality or not, the facts are there, take it as you will. This meaning detachment can be elegiac: in 'Before There Was', about frontier adjustments, the old road lies "like a severed arm/Grown used to its lack of blood", the new climbs "round the bends/Of ownership the war had left", wreckage of war is there, bodies may be, opening out to

At any rate,
For their deaths, a silence passed through us,
All of us held by the sleeping posture of a war.[13]

'Over There; Just Here' has the same alertness, "night-time their shadows light up with ours" in a sort of community, yet for all this "unruffledness" it is an observation post, so "don't point". 'Afterwards' compares animal or jackal cries with human ones as they hover "on the edge/Of the classes of pain"; again, facts need to be realised separately if the justice and rightness of association is to be found; the sounds fade, a human cry is heard, but did the poet "tame" it wrongly now it has "entered into words"; a personal poem not a social one. ACJ's only poem on a wholly Catholic or Christian event is 'Festa', a feat of poised tact, vigilant, observant, reserving judgement:

someone prayed
In a level, finely pitched voice
For the poor, the prisoners, the sick
And unemployed.
. . . .
It was
Soaring and death, on the square
Of San Giovanni, a glimpse at a
Beautiful ceremony.
I lit a cigarette
Thoughtfully, and walked away.[14]

'Where', his classic of the serio-comic, is in "stepped", quasi-trochaic, semi free-verse lines very much ACJ's own, perhaps with a distant forbear in declamations of Mayakovsky, here subtle, factual, fluent, and so well-woven, so integrated, like a strong fine Persian carpet, as to defy unravelling. We can only say it's a kind of agnostic's apology for moonlighting on Yom Kippur, the Day of Atonement, going into gardens, watching a river, reading a paper, awaiting the first star. Embodied in this are signals to ancestry, community, exile, prayer, forgetfulness, change. In fact, an agnostic's piety, "the covenant/That keeps me fasting" coheres in the body of the poem and can't be torn from it.

Mainly, his style is a kind of conversational design, coolly built up, thematically rounded, quick-moving, working by exactness and exclusion: a unity of sound, metre, syntax. Not highly visual or sensory, few metaphors (like Cavafy, thought Robert Friend), never wry, quite a bit of idiom, it acts by clarity. He may offer a fragment, if for Valéryan reasons I know not, but he never overwrites, that chronic deformity of verse today. He was not a virtuoso of language who played at styles to keep a tradition going, he was not an Auden or a Ewart. We feel a central self growing, a provincial reaching out which was never parochialism, each poem shaped to its needs of the moment, like Yeats' stone in the stream "in the midst of all", creating ripples of awareness around it. "No *kuntzim*" (tricks) wrote Robert Friend. And self-effacingly alert to the unsaid:

> The phrases that were meant
> To draw and plead for you
> Only dissect,
>   make you more a stranger,
> Trap.
>   Not everything
>   is grist for poetry,
> Not observation
>   made in place of care.[15]

ACJ's tradition begins, not in linguistics or formalism, rather in the family, whether over-pious ("Granny, look up from your prayer book") or in tragic revelatory seriousness. On his grandmother's death-bed:

> Her God tormented her
> Till, 'Nem Tzu mine neshomme', she cried – 'Take
> Away my soul' . . . .

It wasn't easy getting out of the Tsar's Russia:

> Still, she came through it, my young grandmother,
> And travelled to Manchester,
> Where my grandfather was waiting, with a new language,
> In Cheetham Hill.

> Really, they'd wanted to reach America,
> But never saved enough for the tickets,
> Or perhaps it was just that their hearts were in the east [17]

Lit by sound and flame, 'Grandfather' evokes the Yahrzeit ritual:

> Today, a candle in a glass
> Burns slowly on the mantelpiece.
> Wheesht, the dead are here. [18]

A certain ambivalence, not to be confused with cynicism, what Dan Jacobson[ii] called "your northern, Anglo-Scottish pragmatical self coming down hard on your more emotional Jewish self", attends this inheritance. Jacobs will mock the over-confidence of a Hebrew Lit teacher – "God, girl, your Israel is a ghetto"; this always reminds me, oddly, of Hobsbaum's praise of Leavis, "we laughed at your jokes like children at a treat/But were they jokes?". An old pot is found in an English river with a "half-intelligible Hebrew inscription". A party with brandy, folk-songs, learning, scholarly reminiscence turns from "savouring of inheritance" to "schmaltz" when a record is played. Such is 'Taste'. Glasgow girls in blue skirts are the "religious youth movement", of a mentor he feels that "I was too rough/With his piety", of a teacher he forgets all but black hat, stained beard and "something more I couldn't/Understand in all that legend and recital . . ." A bit of real-life legend occurs when Rashi, great commentator, has his synagogue destroyed in Worms, Nazi Germany. The G.D.R. then rebuilds it exactly as before "So the myth/Was recreated". But some facts are not legend. In cadences of the Song of Solomon, now the darkest of ironies, Jewish girls killed in the Holocaust are remembered. At first this poem's title seems lurid, over-dramatic; when read, it is more than moving, by uniting the public with the personal in a tone of ritual lament it becomes more than a "political poem", and transcends a "committed" one. The Auden of "poetry makes nothing happen" should be made to meditate on this.

Jacobs' sole "real book" of own poems in his lifetime, *The*

Proper Blessing (1976), is, in view of the mass from which it was selected, a work of symmetry, organic and associative. He has on the back a statement on the blessings in Judaism, which, recited on regular or contingent occasions from eating a meal to seeing a rainbow to hearing good or bad news, "praise God for the facts of his creation"; his poems concern living in a world without "certainty" or even "whether one can bless at all". Thus he explores a maze of relativism, evoking or sensing yet never defining certainty. It may be intuitive, as when the "green hills/And weaving lanes/Clear sunsets" of an English-based poem recall Jerusalem: is this "earthly Jerusalem" where he lived long ago or an "earlier Jerusalem" whose images moved him "in this country/Longer ago"? It's vision and memory, but we can't call it dream. In 'Place', without apparent location, a sureness is found, precariously in the sense of both "diaspora/ The long exile burning in us/Burning out" and cross-currents in human relations, for you can talk intimately in the dark

> but in the light
> We don't always say what we have to:
> Our words are not ours.
> Hold me,
> Love, in the light as in darkness,
> As I hold you, in exile,
> Home with you, wherever we are.[19]

Jacobs' most shocking poem, apart from the Holocaust elegy, is perhaps 'A Gloss on Talmud', a gloss on Donne too, with a dash of his colloquialism, stressing incarnation not revelation. "Let's hope each disembodied soul is taught to surmount/Its distaste for this unhappy arrangement". And his most joyful one must be 'My Fathers Planned Me', its poised action the quiet searching eloquence of the true poet, with a dash of defiance:

> But took my love in my arms
> And a found a human music in her voice
> And named as joy what they explored with law. [20]

Thus "we are a new people, she and I". Other namings

rise up to haunt the poet on Hampstead Heath, walking in patches of mud: Hebrew and Yiddish singers, exiles, victims, ironists, lyricists up to "tragic Rosenberg" and beyond. By an opposite, very Arthurian process ACJ reads English history under the clear Jerusalem sky – "When he says "village", I think I feel . . .", and muses on the birth of language, "I wonder/What forms breed here? What language grows?" Yet English-speaking Israeli poets, ignored by politicians and generals, seem to lack a role as non-utilitarian figures in a developing society, while new building in Manchester and in Rosenberg's Whitechapel shows a "furthering of diaspora".

After family, key words in Jacobs are "ghetto" and "diaspora", invoked not just placewise or religiously, also as guides to feeling, relationships, especially of love, and to space, a vital factor:

> You are walking in a country I have never been to
> So I do not know what you have become . . .
> I ask only out of love
> Which gives me over and over your image. [21]

He has this way of opening up areas of silence and distance, then darting in with imaginative audacity. We see in it 'Sound', 'Edinburgh New Town' (quoted), in 'Portrait', reshaping the girl's "image . . . almost", in 'Here', intuiting othernesses, in the Arthurian unLarkinian train of 'O, England' - "The artistry of driving trains . . . Requires a keen eye, which I have not . . . O England, sensed at Apperley Bridge/What powers control you?" His vision of landscape, in this case unscarred by detritus of war (see 'Bab El Wad' and 'Judean Hills') makes the elusive durable just beyond articulation:

> It was these hills in the beginning. . . .
> It was trails over these hills, the first
> Forms.
> . . . . . .   But in the beginning
> Clearly and beyond speech, there were
> These hills. [22]

These are the hills of the world, surely. But it was the wanderings of Abraham that began, in this case, credo and speech:

Long ago the eviction came from God
And he turned towards a dedicated West
Not fleeing, but looking for a land . . .
Only a well or field or cave he dug
Or bought or sowed. He rose early and
Sacrificed, or nearly did, his son. We weep
For this father and his God, and for ourselves
We make his journey thrice a day. [23]

'Earthquake' is displacement of another kind, a rare poem on natural disasters and a humanitarian one:

Our education
Was much taken up with theories of disaster,
"Atrocities"
Became a dulled word in our vocabularies . . .

Old gods of the menace
In thunder and climbing floods, show us how to mourn [24]

In a simpler context, 'South Turkey' shows wit, self-irony at least, *and* compassion on the fraught subject of poverty and begging.

ACJ writes little of "the arts", luckily. We've a poem on Chagall, a painter who appealed to the innovator in Apollinaire, the politics of Lunacharsky, the faith of Maritain and the colourist in Jacobs, with its "lilters", sensory images, even simile, a descriptive lyric of pure joy. His other Chagall, 'Painting', is more thoughtful, meditative, historic, it can be excerpted; this one, 'Painter' needs it all:

We talked of Chagall tonight,
His curved red cow
That almost winks at you,
His lovers planted side by side
In the thick bouquets
Of the dancing villages
Of hard hasidic joy.

Walking home, I couldn't help it,
The moon sailed on a fiddle
In the sky. The traffic lights
Danced green circles over the roofs.
From my feet the ground
Ran into poems the colour
Of this man's fervent world.

And my arms summoned
The climbing lilters of the streets
To a waved Sabbath, fresh as a new calf. [25]

'Mosaic' is a rare poem on mosaic-making as distinct from the glories of Ravenna or Byzantium, playing with the near and the far ("draw near and . . ."), divining it as a metaphor of creative process, of those "terrible gaps of speech". Imagery of Hölderlin is spoken back to its originator, Englished by "your tower", an idea no madder than ACJ's lovely joke for kids, "you like the asterisk best/I told you it was a star": dusty old typewriter not electronic games, it seems. All from the solitary mind scanning the night sky, for

My favourite word is loneliness.
It seems to cry out beyond love's lands
To the night's dark wilderness. [26]

Briefly on the fringes of the Group poets, a subsidiary of the Movement, in the 1950s, Jacobs most admired Martin Bell, praising his generosity, verve, lack of aloofness, and quoting in his slight Scots accent such gems of Bell as "we've been too damned decent" (ah, Orwell), "the old gang born again in young careerists" (yes, 1960), "bully the bourgeois" and, in prose, "Poetry is too popular. What occurred in the Albert Hall was disaster".[iii] That was mischief. On his darker side, he had moral passion; some poems deal with themes of hatred, disdain, disgust, Edgell Rickword's Negative Emotions, inner or outer. "All poets are Jews/Tsvetaeva said./When the fury and spite/Of the loudly virtuous/Build up around me" suggests inner and outer.

A loner with a social conscience, he was not really a satirist, lacking complicity and detachment, probably too emotionally involved. He has early poems on nuclear tests – "Somewhere, near the crouching islands of Japan/Cupped death spilt out . . And no-one died" – and the ruining of the environment by nuclear and other armaments, not propagandist pop-posturing but sad laments for the *heimweh* of the Scottish idyll. He also has a civic conscience, which is harder. Walking home after a booze-up, his group tripping across tramlines "like metal sinews", he hears a medical student speak of a child "as I might speak of a poem/Gone wrong" that it is dying, nothing to do. But in a car accident, the poet knows he'd watch the medic fight for lives; the point, if not the moral, is the split of vocations "that kept our trades apart". A poem on the felling of trees is inadvertently green. "Perhaps it's absurd/To pity trees" yet the valley is now "shamefaced, awkwardly open"; pity and shame go together, a poet's insight. The most alarming of the civic poems, however, is 'What Are You Talking About?'. "Afterwards" there are those who "virtuously" will declare "We didn't know":

It's a familiar sound
To be heard among us now,
The deceiving whine of those
Who participate and know. [27]

Mutism, that active force in art and politics, means we had no power, weren't there, weren't told, or the facts are wrong. His variant reads "to be heard in England now", localising the point; after some hesitation he seems to have chosen the more general "among us now". The extraordinary – or ordinary – thing in his Eichmann poem is its rationalism. Ignoring the usual line about officials obeying orders, or Arendt on the "banality of evil" – Simone Weil, a better activist and finer thinker, is the real source of the idea – Jacobs says simply that the man was a man like us all, sharing the same genetic code, "the cells of that man's brain are divided among us":

Some have its symbols in blue burned into their arms,
Some have a vacancy they will not ever explore . . .
In all of us the bits of brain cry out, cry
For a whole meaning [28]

The evil, the alienation, the difference is that "the mind invades our mind". We must take fragments and give them meaning

For the sake of those who died without meaning.
To us this seems human, to judge
For the sake of those who were denied judgement. [28]

After that, a poem like 'The Real Spite' (untitled) looks harmless enough: spite of a lovers' tiff, literary feud, small betrayal, who knows? It then engages Auden's view that poetry "makes nothing happen", even if a few years earlier he had held that it can "make action urgent and its nature clear", and even if the Spanish War made Auden's 'Spain' happen, affirming however equivocally the free spirit.[iv] Auden's view turns up both in his memorial poem on Yeats – "In the prison of his days/Teach the free man how to praise" – and in his prose essay, *The Public v. The Late Mr W.B. Yeats* where Yeats is accused of vanity, anti-science, proto New Agism, dodgy Nationalism, aristo-peasant poses, a ghastly *Oxford Book* (but re-read the Intro, it's splendid), unconcern with social justice and other patrician follies, then acquitted as a master of language. A superb *jeu d'esprit*, Auden's "trial" is quite unacademic; and into this disputed territory ACJ in his quiet way moves. Something makes poetry happen, Jacobs feels, and his quest for this elusive and alarming factor was his life and art:

Despite the real spite
And making nothing happen
What is it that survives?
. . . .
Something may penetrate
Something inaudible otherwise
May be heard. [29]

There's an element of spite in the dramatic monologue,

'Isaac'; mostly about Ishmael, it's free of the self-regarding poetical interthink which often mars the form. Isaac has suffered from a sacrificial knife at his throat, from his "mocking", knowing, unorthodox brother; Ishmael has suffered from jealousy of the "strength" of a slave girl's child, and been exiled by Abraham, fearful for the inheritance; both (symbolising Israeli and Palestinian) suffer from the passing of the old man and his faith:

> He could do marvellous things; whistle wild songs,
> Climb trees I couldn't, find unknown caves and streams;
> His exploits were legend among our lesser household . . .
>
> I would like to help my brother, but he is still proud.
> There will be no discussion of peace between us;
> And our father, the old God-fearing man, has been
> dead many years. [30]

In 'Israeli Arab', Jacobs meets one whose Hebrew is "better than mine/Will ever be", speaks graceful English, talks "charmingly/Of Nazareth his home town" yet conveys unconsciously a sense of hurt almost entirely by nuances of tone, a politeness "reaching/Towards tones we never seek". The point is made largely by undertones, the overtones matter, but on the surface. Mostly silent, the poet reflects that "I have access to three or four cultures, myself". On another occasion, he reads of an Arab poet "I've never heard of" who will not now be heard: he has been suppressed. Two suggestive allusions, to Auden's "valley of saying" in his Yeats poem, to Empson's many-meanings whereby values are held in equipoise, are invoked to tell this unknown poet to speak out and make it happen:

> And I want to shout:
> Let his poetry survive in its valley
> Making nothing happen,
> Let him demonstrate his types of ambiguity
> Let him speak awkwardly, inadequately,
> Like the rest of us,
> For himself. [31]

In 1993 ACJ wrote from Madrid to me in Riyadh to say he was glad Hebrew is taught in Saudi Arabia, that his translator's interest in "a powerful Hebrew/Arabic cultural mingling in Andalucia, Spain" was strong, and quoted from his poem-in-progress on the Fall of Granada – "the black legend or the rosy one/Which shall I go for?". I thought of `Sol', with its epigraph "*See the sun redden towards evening*":

Near Malaga, I see the sun
Reddening, yellowing into the blue sea
And think of Shlomo Ibn Gabirol,
Malagueñan, who wrote that line.
And this afternoon I drank a cup
Of sweet wine in a hidden square
Where Lorca drank and is remembered . . .

The other end of the Mediterranean,
Where I have also been, fumes. [32]

In T.S. Eliot's sense of an end it was always a beginning:

After a long time in the desert
What is it that brings back poetry
Like water to the Negev?

I don't know. Not virtue
Or debauchery, or any special hardship
Or sudden love.

I'd better, anyhow,
Make the most of it,
And say the proper blessing
For such occasions. [33]

Notes in text:

i. Dannie Abse on Bernard Spencer, quoted by Roger Bowen, *The Edge of a Journey: Notes on Bernard Spencer, London Magazine*, Dec 1979 - Jan 1980, p.96; Dannie Abse, *Poetry Review*, Vol. 85 no.3, Autumn 1995

ii. Quoted by John Rety, *Language of the Heart: A.C.Jacobs, Jewish Chronicle*, Feb 24, 1995

iii. All in *Martin Bell*; *Complete Poems*, Ed. and Intro. Peter Porter, 1988

iv. See C. K. Stead, *Auden's Spain*, *London Magazine*, March 1968, Vol 7, No 12, p.41.

Notes for poems:

1: 'Out', p.32; 2: 'About Making', p.117; 3: 'Private', p.37; 4: 'Untitled' (Up there in Wordsworthshire), p.89; 5: 'Supplication', p.67; 6: 'I Choose Neither', p.71; 7: 'Introduction to a Scottish Sequence', p.66; 8: 'Golders Green Address', p.15; 9: 'Edinburgh New Town', p.113; 10: 'Sound', p.26; 11: 'On a Trip to York', p.58; 12: 'Itzig Manger browses...', p.40; 13: 'Before there was', p.6; 14: 'Festa', 18; 15: 'Lines', p.8; 16: 'Grandmother', p.17; 17: 'Immigration', p.30; 18: 'For My Grandfather', p.3; 19: 'Place', p.111; 20: 'My Fathers Planned Me', p.75; 21: 'For J in Holland', p.84; 22: 'By Kiryat Shemona', p.95; 23: 'Abraham', p.46; 24: 'Earthquake', p.102; 25: 'Painter', p.91; 26: 'For No Words', p.175; 27: 'What Are You Talking About?', p.110; 28: 'Before the Trial of Eichmann', p.7; 29: 'Untitled (Despite the real spite)', p.118; 30: 'Isaac', p.5; 'Israeli Arab', p.97; 32: 'Sol', p.36; 33: 'Return', p.31.

A.C.JACOBS AND HIS MANUSCRIPTS

John Rety

Before Arthur died he wrote me a couple of letters from Spain and, quite unexpectedly, encouraged me to continue with my own writing. He knew that his work meant a lot to me and this was his way, I now conjecture, of passing on some trust, which might give me some assurance at some future date. It is difficult to formulate how I interpret it, but this unasked for encouragement has become very important to me and I suppose gave me the necessary confidence to do the work that had to be done after his death.

I am not much of a traveller but I did go to Madrid to recover whatever manuscripts he'd left behind. Looking back on my journey I realise that without that impetus his work would have probably never been collected.

His friend, Angela Fuertes, was in a state of shock over Arthur's sudden collapse. She came back, tired from work, and found Arthur sitting at the table totally absorbed in writing the introduction to his forthcoming book of translations of Ben-Yitzhak. A few minutes later from another room she heard a tremendous shout and she rushed to see what had happened. She found Arthur slumped on the floor, gasping for breath. She heard him say: "Angela, I'm dying" and saw him go into a coma from which he didn't recover. He died in hospital a few days later.

Angela very kindly let me have photocopies of all the poems he had written in Madrid together with a few bits and pieces he'd brought with him from London. There were some letters and that was all. Except for his spectacles, nothing else of Arthur's could be seen in the flat, not a shirt, not a sock, nothing. As if the man had never lived.

The poems, the new ones, showed a new side to Arthur. He was not just visiting Spain, he was engrossing himself in its problems. Had he survived, he would surely have brought back all that vanished world, the era of Shlomo ibn Gabirol when Jew, Christian and Moor lived together in Spain. He was enthralled by that wisdom and the beauty of "the golden age of Hebrew poetry".

Before Arthur's funeral I made contact with his family who very kindly allowed me to look through his papers and literary remains in Hendon, where he had a small room in his parents' flat.

His room was just like mine, thousands of books and manuscripts piled on top of each other. It took me just under a year to look through the lot. His filing system was the same as mine. The new stuff lay on top of the old.

It soon became obvious that in literary terms he'd left a goldmine. There were countless poems of great strength and purity he had shown nobody before. There were letters to him but only very few copies of letters by him, some letters were started but never finished and certainly not sent. But hundred upon hundred of poems, in notebooks and on bits of paper, copied out by hand repeatedly. His early work in meticulous copperplate handwriting filled many exercise books. He had also developed some kind of shorthand and in later years his handwriting deteriorated. Fortunately he typed out most of the poems he liked. Occasionally he would sign them. Exceptionally he would add the date. Those he dated were very important to him. He wrote poems on backs of programmes and on leaflets and in the fly-leaves of books and diaries. The poem 'Breaking' which appeared in *A Bit of Dialect* he wrote on the back of a Torriano leaflet with a drawing by Jeff Nuttall, while waiting his turn at the New End Theatre during the anti Gulf War protest poetry reading.

Arthur was a frequent visitor to Torriano Meeting House and read there frequently on Sunday evenings. His *A Bit of Dialect* became the first in the Torriano Meeting House Pamphlet series. At the time I assumed that all the poems in it were recently written but some of them had been written over a decade before. 'Out' was published in *The Jewish Chronicle* in 1978 and 'Place', 'Frost' and 'Speech' appeared in *The Scottish Review* of the same year. Only 'Sol', 'Please Note' and 'Private' can be stated with certainty to have been written since about the time I first met him in the late eighties. I typeset the poems while he sat patiently beside me, every now and then lifting a finger to draw attention to a missing comma or a misplaced full stop. He explained how he wanted the broken lines to look, they were mental pauses, a punctuation of sorts. They were not carry overs in a long line, but the same line with a vertical spacing. He read simply, conversationally and was able to be as memorable in sound as in text.

To me everything he wrote is important. Section two of this book contains the best of the poems I found in Arthur's room in Hendon, and the Spanish poems as well as poems previously published only in magazines. No doubt there are some poems which will turn up later. In preparing these notes I have only just found the following fragment (undated, but certainly written in Spain):

> Books disappear. Many people think
> I suppose, they are kept somehow
> In libraries or store-rooms somewhere
> Or cellars or attics. But there are
>
> Plenty of titles that have just vanished,
> You couldn't find them anywhere. For instance
> A History of the Jews in Ireland.

There are of course others, exercises from the age eleven onwards, early pieces that I feel Arthur would not have wanted published, even though here and there a phrase jumps out and everything becomes memorable. Once this book is published, I'm sure other work will come to light. Especially letters. Perhaps they contain Arthur as much as his poems.

A final word on how I estimate him. In my opinion A.C.Jacobs is an English poet. His subject matter and his origins are secondary. We are all, every one of us, of mixed antecedents. For me A.C.Jacobs is saying something which can be said only in the precision of the English language. As a poet – perhaps a major one – he may well be the last of his kind. He wrote in a language that nobody speaks any more. It is a language of true feeling and whenever I use it with the flat determination it requires I'm asked unerringly "where do you come from?". A.C.Jacobs himself replied Vilna:"A bit east of the Gorbals,/In around the heart".

Arthur was of course an outstanding translator. But if you want to find A.C.Jacobs go straight to the poems. Once read they'll stay with you forever.

A.C.JACOBS

Anthony Rudolf

There was a man. And then there was not a man. He was alive. And then he was not.

His body and mind were in our world. And then they were not.

What we call his remains were brought to these holy grounds last year. They were placed in the grave. Prayers were spoken. All shared the responsibility of covering the coffin with earth.

Today the tombstone is raised. A trace of the man is written in stone, his name, his good name, Arthur Jacobs – Arthur Jacobs, the poet who chose to be known as A.C.Jacobs.

The man loved his family. The man loved his friends. The man loved words. His family loved this man. His friends, women and men, loved this man. Traces of the man remain in the hearts of all who loved him.

Words too loved this man, even if they were not always very friendly. But he made great demands on them, and they made even greater demands on him. How could he not? How could they not? We are talking about poetry, the very life blood of the language. To say you have written a poem is to say you are in the company of – to name a few poets he loved – Isaac Rosenberg, Ibn Gabirol, David Vogel, Garcia Lorca. This is a responsibility.

Sometimes words made him angry, as a child or a spouse or a parent or a lover makes you angry, but he worked hard on them and on himself, and he was not angry any more. Until the next time. This was a marriage, an agon. Language was his bride. His *Shekhina*. In life Arthur sheltered under the shadow of the wing of the *Shekhina*, just as he does in death.

Arthur was Arthur, a private individual, a person alone as we all are. But we are not, as it were, *only* alone. For Arthur, the pressure of history and geography on experience were crucial, visceral. The tension between his Jewishness and his

Scottishness was palpable; his inner identity struggle was not some fashionable foray into ethnicity, but a matter of spiritual life, and had been so since he was a young man, and would remain so till the end. It was not a question of either/or, rather what does it mean to live both? This involved the wider questions of Jewish and Israel, Scottish and Britain. Poetry demanded of him that he live this struggle. The struggle demanded of him that he live as a poet. His life as a man was a dialectical process incarnate.

He did not only live his struggle in London or in English, for he spent several years in Israel and he returned to the Scotland of his childhood – and he made the most of the great multi-ethnic metropolis we inhabit. He was a translator of several cultures and languages, notably Hebrew but also Yiddish. Now he too is translated, into a language the living do not speak.

Latterly he lived in Spain with a good friend. There he thought often of the Golden Age, the time long gone when Christian, Jew and Muslim lived in harmony, as they have done in Sarajevo till recently. He had earlier translated Moses Ibn Ezra, one of the great Hebrew poets of Spain. He prayed in his own way for reconciliation between Isaac and Ishmael in the Land; he prayed that Jerusalem, a city he loved, would truly be a city of peace.

And it was in Spain that the bride of language – the heartof poetry and love – was vanquished, as she always is, by the bride of death. But Arthur was a true poet. And the traces of true poets live on after their death, like their children, *as* their children. These children indeed can survive for generations. Some of the poems and translations of *our* friend will surely do just that. And this is the only consolation for those who survive. That he, like the loved poets named earlier, died before his time is no longer the point.

There was a man. And then there was not a man.

He was alive. And then he was not.

(*Speech at A.C.Jacobs' Tombstone Setting, Rainham, March 19, 1995*)

LIST OF POEMS

Where poems are 'Untitled', this list gives the first line in inverted commas. If the title is 'Poem' the first line is added.

POEMS PUBLISHED IN BOOK FORM

POEMS UNCOLLECTED IN BOOK FORM/ UNCOLLECTED POEMS

TRANSLATIONS FROM THE HEBREW PUBLISHED IN BOOK FORM

David Vogel

Avraham Ben-Yitzhak

TRANSLATIONS UNCOLLECTED IN BOOK FORM AND UNPUBLISHED TRANSLATIONS

OTHER POEMS